THE DIVORCE

THE DIVORCE HANDBOOK

Fiona Shackleton
and
Olivia Timbs

Thorsons
An Imprint of HarperCollins*Publishers*

To our families

Thorsons
An Imprint of HarperCollins*Publishers*
77–85 Fulham Palace Road,
Hammersmith, London W6 8JB

Published by Thorsons 1992
1 3 5 7 9 10 8 6 4 2

A catalogue record for this book
is available from the British Library

ISBN 0 7225 2704 7

Typeset by Harper Phototypesetters Limited
Northampton, England
Printed in Great Britain by
Hartnolls Ltd, Bodmin, Cornwall

CONTENTS

Foreword		7
Introduction		9
1.	Until divorce us do part: the past, the present and the future	11
2.	Is divorce really necessary?	15
3.	Finding a good solicitor	18
4.	What solicitors can do for you	23
5.	Basic law and divorce procedure	26
6.	How to help your solicitor	37
7.	What may happen during divorce proceedings	41
8.	Arrangements when there are no children	49
9.	Practical arrangements for children	63
10.	Financial arrangements for children	74
11.	Retirement and death: pensions, life assurance and wills	84
12.	Other financial arrangements: chattels, trusts and family companies	93
13.	Misapprehensions	100
14.	Appearing in court	107
15.	Legal costs – and who foots the bill?	115
16.	Are you entitled to legal aid?	122
17.	Cohabitation and pre-marriage contracts	132
18.	Divorce in Northern Ireland and Scotland; and when a divorce should take place abroad	136
19.	Do-it-yourself divorce	143
20.	Divorce may not be the end	146
21.	Nullity of marriage	155

22. Reconciliation and conciliation   157
     Appendix A: Acts of Parliament   163
     Appendix B: Glossary of legal terms, and sample
     petition form   165
     Appendix C: Further reading and useful addresses   168
     Index   171

FOREWORD

When a potential client contacts me initially, the problems he or she faces – such as how to begin divorce proceedings, what solicitors can and cannot do, and the financial costs involved – are frequently common to every case, and have simple answers. Over the years I have often been asked whether there was a suitable, simple guide to help someone contemplating divorce, so when Olivia (whose own divorce I handled some years ago) asked me if I would be interested in writing this book with her, I readily agreed in the hope that those who read it could be spared undue anxiety (and expense) and get the information they need in order to take informed and knowledgeable decisions.

The legal profession is steadily moving away from a confrontational approach to divorce and family matters, and lawyers are well situated to play a positive and constructive role at the time of a marital breakdown. I hope that this book will help show you how you can best work with your lawyer to achieve an acceptable separation, and set a framework for any future relationship. It often takes an enormous amount of courage to ask questions about divorce proceedings, and I hope that having the answers to hand in this book will benefit those who need it most.

Between the time of initial idea for this book and its execution, Olivia and I have both had two children, and I continue to work full-time. Olivia has been responsible for transforming my random thoughts culled from some years of practical experience into a readily digestible text, stripping away as much legal jargon as possible. She has also been responsible for assembling all the non-legal information essential for someone experiencing marriage breakdown.

I am therefore hugely grateful to her, and to my Partners at Farrer & Co., particularly Richard Griffiths and Robert Clinton for their advice and for allowing me the time and giving me the support I needed. The divorce team at Farrers, who have helped us so willingly have been wonderful, particularly Simon Bruce, my invaluable assistant, my Partner, Richard Parry, and his assistant, Sian Blore. John Dewar, our legal Director of Training, has kindly helped enormously, as has Richard Anelay of Counsel. Thanks are also due to Caroline O'Dwyer of the Legal Aid office, and to Anne Dunne in Dublin and David Adams in Edinburgh for their invaluable advice on Chapter 18. My secretary, Ione Noble, has not only been responsible for handing me the right bit of the book at the right time, having proof-read it, but has organized me so that while the book was being written I was able to continue to give clients the service they needed, and for that I am also indebted to her.

Fiona Shackleton
April, 1992

$\mathscr{I}$NTRODUCTION

When I started divorce proceedings I wanted to know what I was letting myself in for legally. I wanted to read something that would give me an idea of the procedures involved, but although I hunted in a number of bookshops all I could find were paperbacks on the emotional aspects of separation.

I was advised to consult Fiona Shackleton at Farrers. I was in luck; I liked her style and I liked her personally. My divorce was straightforward, because my former husband and I were young and we had no children. Our assets were tied up in our house and there were no major problems in dividing the capital. Nevertheless there were moments when I felt so angry that I wanted my husband to suffer financially, but Fiona explained the fruitlessness of that route. So, thanks to her, my divorce went through as smoothly as could be hoped and the decree absolute was granted nine months after the petition was filed.

Fiona provided the answers to all my questions, but all along I wished there had been a book available which would have saved her time (and our money). A couple of years later I suggested to Fiona that Farrers produce a short book which we would write together, outlining the legal procedures and explaining what couples could expect during a divorce. They agreed to the project, Thorsons publishers thought it was worth supporting, and this book is the result.

First and foremost Fiona and I hope that after you have read this book you will decide that divorce is *not* the best solution for you and your spouse, particularly if you have dependent children. Please do not jeopardize their futures unless you are absolutely sure that there is no way you can stay together. Can you wait until your youngest child is 16? You will still have at least 30 years left to build separate lives. If one couple with children decide not to divorce after reading this book, it will have been worth writing.

However, if divorce is inevitable this handbook will give a flavour of the divorce process by examining how it affects couples in reality and not just in theory. It is not designed to be comprehensive but rather a clear, straightforward and easy-to-understand description of the stages of divorce.

This book will help you to find good lawyers, and explains how to use them effectively; it will take you step by step through the legal process, tell you what is likely to happen to your assets (your house and car, for example) and how your pension entitlement may be affected; it will also give you a good indication of what arrangements may be made for your children – from where they live, to who pays for their school socks and what religious education they may have.

It will explain who pays the legal costs, and tell you whether or not you are entitled to legal aid; it will also explain the common misapprehensions that men and women are under when they start divorce proceedings. It will describe how the conciliation service works, suggest other people you might like to consult during and after your divorce, and explain what protection people have who split up after cohabiting. Throughout the book Fiona and I have drawn upon real case studies to illustrate the various procedures – in all cases the names of the participants have been changed to protect their privacy.

The use of technical legal terms has been kept to a minimum (although there is a comprehensive glossary at the back of the book), and we recommend that if you have any further questions about any terms you ask your own solicitor about them. Throughout the laws and procedures described are those effective in England and Wales; a special chapter has been devoted to Northern Irish and Scottish law, although anyone undergoing divorce proceedings in Northern Ireland or Scotland will need more advice than there has been space to provide here.

I hope this handbook will provide answers to some of the problems that can develop during divorce proceedings, and will outline the circumstances that may lead to bitterness and arguments between you and your spouse.

Finally, because by reading this book you will have a much clearer idea of what is likely to happen when you step into a solicitor's office, Fiona and I hope that it will make a necessarily gloomy and difficult period in your life a little more bearable.

Olivia Timbs
April, 1992

1

UNTIL DIVORCE US DO PART

The past, the present and the future

In 1990, over 190,000 divorce petitions were filed in England and Wales – a 4 per cent increase over the previous year – and over 150,000 decrees absolute were granted. Divorce now involves nearly 1 per cent of the adult population every year. The parents of one in every four children under 16 will divorce; ten years ago this figure was one in five. A staggering 43 per cent of parents who no longer look after their children daily (mainly fathers) lose touch completely – 750,000 British children never see their fathers. In 1989, 10,000 sets of parents went to court to battle over arrangements for their children. Legal aid expenditure in divorce and family proceedings in courts totalled over £141 million in 1990–91, and that figure does not include the millions spent by people who used solicitors privately.

These grim statistics are only part of the picture. Studies have shown that divorced people are more likely to contract chronic illnesses and die at an earlier age than people who remain married. The children of divorced couples do less well at school, are likely to be more aggressive and disobedient; those who live with a step-parent suffer even more. About 10 per cent of parents regret divorcing. And yet, divorce continues to be ever more popular, taking its financial and emotional toll.

There are a number of factors to account for the massive jump in the divorce rate in this country over the last 20 years: changes in the divorce law, wider availability of legal aid, the fact that people live longer, and the fact that divorce is no longer the social stigma that it was earlier this century. People now have higher expectations of marriage and there has been a shift away from the duties of marriage to the rights of individuals within marriage.

This is reflected in the number of women who petition for divorce. Although they are most likely to suffer financially as a result of divorce and may have to support their children on state benefit, they are much more likely to start divorce proceedings than their husbands – irrespective of their socio-economic class. The majority (89 per cent) of two-parent families rely mainly on one or both parents' earnings; 66 per cent of single parent families rely on social security benefits.

In the past, divorce was really only feasible for the very rich. Now, legal aid has enabled even those people in the poorest circumstances to divorce, and their numbers have made a significant impact on the divorce rate over the last 30 years.

A stable society, reflected by marriage and cohesive families, is crumbling, according to some people, who also hold that divorce is now too easy. Other people believe that if divorce were less acrimonious and disputes over children, money and property were minimized, broken families would not suffer so much in the long term and society would not be so threatened.

A different view is put forward by Laurence Stone, former Professor of History at Princeton University in the United States. He argues that divorce, in some senses, is replacing death as the conventional means of ending a marriage. In *Road to Divorce, England 1530-1987* he points out that in the nineteenth century, about 30 per cent of marriages ended prematurely because of the death of one spouse. The same percentage (roughly one in three marriages), in the latter part of the twentieth century, ends because of divorce.

Whether you believe that divorce is already too easy, too acrimonious or simply a reflection of developments in society, there is a consensus that current divorce law is muddled and in need of an overhaul.

In the early part of this century, divorce could only take place if someone was found to be at fault. As a result, divorced people were a social liability: one side was to blame, while the injured party would become an outcast. Fortunately, these attitudes have changed for the most part.

The Divorce Reform Act of 1969, on which current divorce law is based, led to a doubling of the divorce rate in the early 1970s. Irretrievable breakdown of the marriage is now the sole ground for divorce. However, you still have to give the details of why the marriage has broken down, in accordance with one of five facts: your spouse's adultery, your spouse's utterly unreasonable behaviour, because you have been deserted for two years, because you and your spouse have lived apart for two years (when you both agree to divorce) or for five years (when your spouse does not agree to divorce). In other words, divorce law is a muddle of no-fault and blame – depending on which of these five facts is cited.

When the legislation came into effect in the seventies it was thought that the factors where blame could be apportioned (i.e. adultery, desertion and unreasonable behaviour) would slowly fade away and that most people would opt for separation. This idea backfired. Only about a quarter of divorce petitions are after a two- or five-year separation – three-quarters are still fault-based.

Once divorce is on the cards, few people want to wait for two years before they are free of their spouse. Some people want to remarry as soon as possible. When adultery or unreasonable behaviour is cited in divorce, the average length of the proceedings is only five months. And, like it or not, many people still want to blame their spouse or a third party for the breakdown of their marriage. It is rare for a divorce to take place by mutual consent.

As the majority of petitioners are women who often feel vulnerable, both economically and emotionally, they want to have the divorce sorted out relatively quickly, and therefore continue to choose one of the factors where blame is apportioned. (Interestingly, adultery is most frequently cited by people from the professions, unreasonable behaviour by women in the poorest circumstances.)

In addition, whatever may be believed by divorce law reformers in favour of guilt-free divorce, most people need some focus for their bitterness. And surely it is better for the anger to be enshrined in the divorce proceedings than for it to be manifest through squabbles over money or over the children? So, in defence of current law, it does at least provide a way of venting ill feelings.

However, the legislation has many other shortcomings. As the law stands at present a decree absolute can be obtained without any decision being made over how the couple's finances will be organized; either party can also remarry before the final financial settlement is made. The current law is also weak where children are concerned: there is no longer any compulsion for the parent who looks after the children to attend court to answer questions on where they are going to live, who is going to look after them, and where they are going to go to school (the District Judge will only require the attendance of one or both parents if he thinks the arrangements have been inadequately explained on the form which accompanies the Petition). In addition, the present system provides no support for marriages that have a chance of survival, and the entire procedure is still embarrassing and sometimes humiliating.

Late in 1990 the Law Commission published a major report advocating that there should be further changes in the law to reduce the bitterness, to emphasize the resolution of the tricky issues of children, finances and property, and to introduce a cooling-off period before a decree absolute could be granted.

The Law Commission proposed to take the blame out of proceedings completely. Either the husband or wife would be able to file an application for divorce, and after 12 months either of them could apply to make the divorce absolute, without any need to specify the grounds. This suggestion would make some divorce proceedings longer, and before the decree could be granted the family's finances and arrangements for the children would have to be sorted out. At the moment divorce procedure is separate, legally, from money and children. The chief benefit of this proposal is that it would integrate them.

This reform would have one particularly important implication: people would have to look at the practical realities of divorce at the very beginning of proceedings, and it might also slow down the divorce rate.

But these proposals are likely to have a bumpy ride through Parliament – if the Government ever attempts to introduce legislation based on them. There will no longer be any grounds for divorce – it will just be a question of waiting. And, as the Lord Chancellor has said, there are people who feel that some form of matrimonial fault should still be at the root of all the law.

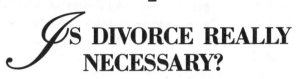

2
IS DIVORCE REALLY NECESSARY?

WHEN YOUR MARRIAGE IS AT AN ALL-TIME LOW

Divorce solicitors are often at their busiest in the New Year and during September. They are inundated with people who have decided that divorce is the only answer to the problems in their marriages; those who found that the strain of spending Christmas or the summer holidays with a reluctant spouse was too much to bear, and those who find the prospect of having to be polite to in-laws again impossible.

The hairline cracks that began to appear some time ago suddenly spring open and one or other utters the fateful words 'I think we should separate.' But to go straight to a solicitor at this stage may not be appropriate, and may make your relationship even more tense.

With luck, the relationship will not have soured completely and you still might have a chance of reconciliation and re-building your marriage. If you think there is a possibility of a future together, solicitors are not the people to approach. Read Chapter 22 about marriage guidance and other support services first.

Whether you go ahead with the divorce or you manage to salvage your marriage, you will need emotional and psychological support. This may seem so obvious that it is not worth saying, but there are a great number of people, men in particular, who go to a solicitor without talking to anyone else first – let alone their partners. At best this is a complete waste of money. While you may hope that a solicitor will give you advice, because he or she has so much experience of divorcing couples, solicitors are not trained to provide that support. Why call out the plumber when you need an electrician?

You may find your friends and family can help you. If you find that impossible and you cannot turn to someone neutral, for example at your local church, it is far better to go to your GP and ask to be referred to a counsellor or psychotherapist for advice than to waste money going to see a solicitor.

DO YOU REALLY WANT OR NEED TO DIVORCE?

Talking to friends or a counsellor may help disentangle your muddled feelings and enable you and your spouse to sort out a life together. While the relationship may seem doomed emotionally, you should understand that divorce may not make you any happier; it will certainly make your life more complicated and it could make it a great deal unhappier. Even so, it may be the lesser of two evils.

If you are rich, with unlimited liquid assets, or you are young with a good chance of marrying again and you have no children, divorce may be the answer for you. People who do not fit into either of these categories (and who are not in physical danger from their spouse) should read this handbook carefully before embarking on divorce. Divorce is no panacea.

Advantages and disadvantages

Draw up a list of what you think may be the advantages of divorce. You will probably find that they are emotional in nature, mostly to do with the relationship with your spouse and negative – i.e. divorce offers an escape from a terrible situation:

- You have met someone else
- You argue constantly (which must damage your children)
- Your spouse drinks and/or gambles
- Your spouse beats you up
- Your spouse is too possessive
- Your spouse nags all the time
- Your spouse will not let you go out on your own
- Your spouse has been unfaithful once too often
- You no longer have anything in common, other than your children

The disadvantages of divorce are primarily of a more practical nature and are to do with your children:

- Your children want both their parents there, even when they argue
- You cannot see your children whenever you want to
- It will be difficult to bear the fact that your spouse's new partner is bringing up your children
- It will be difficult to bear the fact that another person has taken away your husband
- Divorce proceedings are expensive

- You will not have as much money after the divorce as you had before it: one income cannot easily support two households
- You will still argue about money and your children
- You will be lonely

These lists are not comprehensive, and you will be able to produce your own list which will help you decide whether, on balance, you really do want to divorce.

Unless you gain great personal insight and self-knowledge through your divorce, you may not be any happier in the years to come. While there is a chance that you will meet and share your life with someone else, you will still have to deal with your former spouse and share the responsibility for looking after your children.

If you then have regrets it will be too late, and you will be worse off emotionally, as well as financially. Surveys of divorced people reveal that a significant proportion wish they had never divorced in the first place.

So, before you embark on divorce proceedings, do explore all the alternatives – there may be a less costly option that you have not considered.

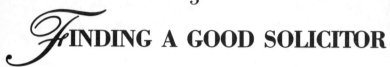

3

FINDING A GOOD SOLICITOR

When you have explored all the alternatives, and you finally decide that divorce is inevitable, you will need a solicitor. You may want to do the divorce by yourselves, particularly if you have no children and you are in agreement on how your assets should be split – in the way that many people now tackle the conveyancing themselves when they are buying and selling property. If you do, read Chapter 19 on Do-it-yourself divorce.

Most people will need to consult a solicitor if divorce proceedings are inevitable. The trouble is, as one barrister with extensive experience of legal aid work candidly said, a great number of solicitors do not know enough about divorce and advise their clients badly.

A second-rate solicitor can leave you with an unfair financial settlement and/or irrevocably sour the relationship between you and your spouse by causing unnecessary arguments and running up huge costs which you and your spouse have to pay from your joint assets.

HOW YOU FIND A SOLICITOR

There are a number of options when looking for a solicitor:

- Through the firm that acts for your company
- Using the solicitor who handled the conveyancing when you bought your flat or house
- A personal recommendation
- From the Solicitors Family Law Association
- County courts (listed in the telephone directory under 'Courts')
- Citizens Advice Bureaux – listed in the telephone directory
- Yellow Pages – see under 'Legal Services' and 'Solicitors'

Businessmen and -women have a head start here. The firm of solicitors that acts for your company should not be forgotten, even though you may think that it is a bad idea to mix your personal life with your professional one. While commercial lawyers may not have a strong matrimonial department, if you have a reasonable relationship with one of the partners, he or she should be able to recommend either an individual or a firm that specializes in that area.

Many women, however, have only limited contact with solicitors. They may have only come across one when they were buying and selling property or drawing up a will, or when a member of their family died. And while the solicitor you have used in the past may have a partner experienced in matrimonial matters, it may be a good idea to look further afield. In addition, if the solicitor has acted for both you and your spouse in the past, the firm may have a policy of refusing matrimonial work that necessarily affects you both.

Another good starting point is a friend who has been through a divorce: a personal recommendation is often the best. But what suits him or her may not suit you – you may want to fight your spouse for every penny you can get hold of, while your friend's solicitor may have a rather more conciliatory style.

If you are unable to explore any of these options, your next best bet is to approach The Solicitors Family Law Association. This organization has 2,000 members in England and Wales who are bound by a code of practice to try to settle a divorce as amicably as possible. A list is available from The Solicitors Family Law Association (address and contact person are given in Appendix C).

County courts (listed in the telephone directory under 'Courts') have a list of solicitors who use that court. The clerk of the divorce section may be able to suggest a few reputable local firms rather than give you a long list.

You can also find the names of solicitors through Citizens Advice Bureaux, your local library and the Yellow Pages. CABs and libraries have copies of The Law Society's Regional Directories, which will tell you the names of solicitors in your area and the type of work they do.

HOW TO PICK A GOOD SOLICITOR

When choosing your solicitor it is best to consider the following criteria:

- Always choose a specialist
- Choose someone you like personally

- Choose a solicitor whose reputation you respect
- Be prepared to question the solicitor closely before you commit yourself

You may decide to consult a solicitor for some general advice before you embark on full divorce proceedings, or you may need to consult a solicitor about your financial affairs long before divorce is on the cards. Either occasion can be a good opportunity to find out about the solicitor and whether or not he or she would suit you if you do embark on divorce.

A handful of solicitors' firms offer a 'fixed fee interview' where you will be given up to half an hour's advice for £5 – which may be perfect if you only want general advice and you are unlikely to have a divorce. But you are more likely to meet a less experienced solicitor than a senior partner, and the best firms do not need to offer such a service to attract clients.

It is perfectly in order to 'shop around' for a solicitor. Make a number of appointments with different firms until you find a lawyer you like. But be prepared to pay between £40 and £100 for your first half-hour with each one.

Most importantly, make sure that the solicitor you consult comes from a firm which has at least one partner specializing in family work full-time. You are most likely to find these firms in London and there are about half a dozen who are known for their matrimonial work, and you can usually find an expert in most cities and big towns.

The solicitors who do not know their stuff are generally part-time matrimonial lawyers who dabble with this sort of work. They may give you an adequate service if you and your spouse are in complete agreement about all your affairs, and only need a lawyer to help you through the basic legal procedure. If there are any arguments, do make sure that the person you consult will ensure you make the best arrangements – and that does not only mean financial ones.

Solicitors who are members of The Solicitors Family Law Association should in theory know quite a bit about divorce, but they do not necessarily spend all their working hours on Family matters and there is no guarantee that members of the Association will have that much experience in divorce.

It is important that you like the solicitor you choose. However highly recommended an individual solicitor is, and regardless of the fact that he or she seems to offer the service you are looking for, do not pick him or her if you do not feel comfortable. You may have to divulge many intimate details to your solicitor in the course of the divorce, and if you instinctively feel ill at ease you will find the divorce process completely unbearable.

So, if you think the solicitor is too young and inexperienced and will not support you sufficiently, or too old and out of touch with your generation, or you would prefer a woman or a young man, go elsewhere.

Try to discover what reputation the solicitor has: finding the right solicitor for you will make all the difference to your experience of divorce. For example, at the extremes, pick a solicitor who has a reputation as a conciliator if you want a gentle ride and a fighter when you are prepared to or want to battle with your spouse. Most good solicitors can adapt to suit your needs.

You may prefer to stay on good terms with your spouse, in which case briefing a 'fighter' who bullies him or her to part with an extra £10,000, creating bad feelings that sour discussions over your children's education for years, could be a big mistake.

Choosing the right solicitor can have implications far beyond your divorce proceedings. For example, couples who have been married for many years will probably have many mutual friends and both are likely to want to continue to see them. Try to avoid alienating friends by forcing them to take sides if your solicitor starts making unreasonable demands on your behalf. Your friends may take pity on your spouse and decide not to see you, which could be the end of a valuable support network.

Do not be afraid of asking some penetrating questions about the solicitor when you first meet. One who seems reluctant to answer your questions may not suit you, in which case you should find one who is more open.

Questions to ask the solicitor

When you first go along to a solicitor, make sure to ask some pertinent questions – after all, you are the client, it is you who should be interviewing him or her, and not the other way round!

- How long have you been doing matrimonial work?
- Do you act mainly for husbands or wives? (The best handle both so that they keep in touch with the attitudes of men and women – some

women might find a woman solicitor most sympathetic; others may feel that an older man will provide them with the best support.)
- Do you have a reputation as a fighter or are you conciliatory?
- What percentage of cases do you win if they end up in court?
- How much do you charge?
- How much will it all cost?
- Who will have to pay?
- How long will it take?

Do not always feel obliged to follow your solicitor's advice or be afraid to restrain your solicitor's enthusiasm if you think that will make relations between you and your spouse impossible. For example, your solicitor may recommend that your husband's bank account be frozen so that he cannot take his assets out of the country, but you might feel that this is unnecessarily aggressive. Remember, the solicitor is there to follow your instructions.

A solicitor is obliged to tell you whether or not you are entitled to legal aid for your costs in divorce proceedings. Some firms do not handle any legal aid work but will recommend the name of a solicitor who does.

When you decide to use a lawyer who will charge you full costs even though you would be entitled to legal aid, you will have to find the money out of your eventual settlement. A solicitor who fails to tell you that you are entitled to legal aid will have to forego his or her fees if this oversight is discovered.

HOW TO CHANGE SOLICITORS

There may be circumstances where you fall out with your solicitor in the middle of divorce proceedings. You may feel that your solicitor acted inappropriately or divulged information that you expressly told him or her not to and you therefore want to consult someone different.

In extreme cases, you may want to complain about the way your solicitor has treated you. If it is a relatively minor matter, say, your letters and telephone calls are never answered, take it up with the partner in the firm who is responsible for matrimonial work, or the senior partner.

If you want an independent view about your treatment contact the Legal Practice Information Department at The Law Society (address given in Appendix C). Formal complaints should be put in writing and sent to the Solicitors' Complaints Bureau (address given in Appendix C).

4
*W*HAT SOLICITORS CAN DO FOR YOU

A good lawyer will ask you at your first meeting whether or not you should really be there. Of course, if you are just asking general advice and want some explanation of the divorce procedure and options available, that is fine.

They are right to remind you to ask yourself whether or not your marriage is really over and divorce is inevitable. Have you really tried your best to talk it over together? As we mentioned in Chapter 2, many people still rush off to a lawyer when they should be seeing a marriage guidance counsellor or a therapist and when there is still time and opportunity for reconciliation. You may think that the problems between you are too major to put right; however, often small changes can make a marriage work again.

If you are convinced your marriage is over and little can be done to help heal the wounds, but you still have a few outstanding concerns, you may think a lawyer with many years' experience of family work will give you the sort of advice you want and think is right for you.

Beware: do not confuse legal advice with emotional advice. While the best lawyers will become well-tuned to their clients' emotional needs they are not trained to deal with them, and even when they offer advice it may not be the right advice for you.

Secondly, legal time is expensive, and it is a waste of money if you use your top London lawyer as a counsellor at £175 per hour, which will ultimately have to come from a share of your joint assets.

WHAT SOLICITORS CAN DO FOR YOU
Solicitors are there to give independent advice and to minimize the bitterness and difficulties that may develop between you and your spouse. Your solicitor should not make matters more complicated than necessary – you will only have to pay him or her to unscramble the resulting muddle.

- They can take you through the divorce process and make sure all the legal paperwork is completed correctly (see Chapter 5).
- They can help you sort out your financial affairs (see Chapters 7 and 8) and make sure the arrangements between you and your spouse for looking after your children are in their best interest (see Chapters 9 and 10). Protracted litigation over both money and children can be very expensive. A good solicitor will impress on you the importance of agreeing with your spouse and, particularly in cases where children will be affected, any agreement is better for them than having some arrangements imposed on you by a judge. Good solicitors will advise you on the best way to split your capital assets. They will help you decide whether maintenance or a clean break is the best option for you, taking into account the amount of tax you may have to pay. Depending on your financial circumstances they will make sure you do not lose out on your spouse's pension, or they will explain how you may be entitled to certain social security benefits.
- If you are not going to divorce, solicitors can only offer advice – not action – concerning your financial position, as any arrangements you decide to make in any circumstances other than divorce are not watertight. If your separation arrangement does not work out, all financial matters will have to be renegotiated between you and your spouse, as the courts can have no powers outside full divorce proceedings. Even those arrangements recorded in a formal separation agreement are completely open to variation by the court in the context of divorce proceedings instigated by either party at any time (see Chapter 7 on separation agreements).
- Solicitors are *essential* if there is any disagreement between you and your spouse on arrangements for your children and your financial affairs.

WHAT SOLICITORS CANNOT DO FOR YOU

Solicitors should *not* help you over these matters:

- If you are still at the stage of 'should I/shouldn't I divorce?', do not expect your solicitor to make up your mind for you.
- While a solicitor can help you through the legal maze, do not expect him or her to give you emotional advice. Of course, so much of a divorce

is emotionally loaded that many decisions you make will have an emotional element. Just make sure you never find yourself in a position of making a decision, regretting it and then turning on your solicitor and saying 'But you told me to do that.'

Sarah, for example, discovered that she was pregnant just after she started divorce proceedings on the grounds of her husband Tom's adultery. They already had two children, and before she told Tom about the pregnancy she rang up her lawyer to ask whether or not she should have an abortion.

Even though there are implications in this for the amount of money she would receive, her lawyer could not advise her on those grounds. Whether or not you have an abortion can only be a personal and emotional decision.

Many lawyers will tell you stories about clients who make unreasonable demands on them but who have to be given time because they are calling the tune. One 48-year-old woman found the divorce procedure so fraught that she rang her lawyer at 3 a.m. and spent over half an hour threatening suicide.

Other people forget that divorce is a legal process. John, with three teenage children, filed for divorce on the grounds of his wife Joanna's adultery. It soon became clear that he did not really want a divorce – he was using it as a threat to force Joanna to heel: 'I want her back, whatever the cost,' he announced the third time he met his lawyer.

By then, his action had so alienated her that there was no hope for the marriage; his chance to save it, when he first discovered she had been unfaithful, was lost because he marched off to a lawyer instead of trying to discuss it with her.

Melanie accepted reluctantly that her marriage was over. She had a reasonable relationship with her husband Mark, who lived near and helped look after their two children, spending more time with them than many of their friends' fathers in supposedly stable marriages. The problem was Anna, the woman with whom Mark now lived. What could Melanie's lawyer do to protect Mark against the folly of marrying Anna after the divorce? The answer was: nothing.

There are both limits to the legal process and limits to what lawyers may advise: stick to the law and you will be most satisfied with your lawyer's performance. Ask questions beyond his or her remit and you will be disappointed. Solicitors cannot take emotional responsibility for you.

5

ℬASIC LAW AND DIVORCE PROCEDURE

Now to some of the nitty gritty. You have chosen your solicitor and whether or not you are on good terms with your spouse, there is no chance of saving your marriage. Divorce proceedings are starting and you want to know what will they involve.

In theory, the divorce itself should not cause any major problems because the mechanics are straightforward. In practice, divorces become messy and long-drawn out because both parties are unable or unwilling to resolve some of the practical problems: where to live, what arrangement will be made for the children, and how to sort out their finances.

This chapter deals with the legal steps in divorce – discussion of the messy practical problems comes later. It will give you a rough timetable for a divorce which goes through without any hitches, and when both parties agree that the marriage is over, covering the following topics:

- When can a divorce take place?
- What are grounds for divorce?
- The paperwork:
  Filing a petition
  Acknowledgement
  Application for decree nisi and preparing the affidavit
  Application for decree absolute
  Decree nisi

(See page 36 for a summary table of the paperwork and time scale involved in straightforward proceedings, and Appendix B for a sample petition form.)

WHEN CAN A DIVORCE TAKE PLACE?

A divorce can only take place in England and Wales if the parties have been married for a year; you or your spouse must have been living in

England or Wales for the previous year, or have your permanent home there. It does not matter where the marriage took place originally. (If you and your spouse both agree that your marriage was a mistake on your honeymoon you can apply for a judicial separation when you get home. See Chapter 7, page 46. We discuss divorce in Scotland and Northern Ireland in Chapter 18).

Under current divorce legislation neither party can be blamed for the breakdown of a marriage. Nevertheless a reason for its collapse must be shown – the grounds for the divorce – and some grounds do carry overtones of guilt. The law is constructed in such a way that one side has to file the petition for divorce, and becomes the petitioner, and the other side becomes the respondent.

WHAT ARE GROUNDS FOR DIVORCE?

The only grounds for divorce are irretrievable breakdown of the marriage, but the petition has to outline one of five facts which can be established as a fact and which the district judge (a judge) is satisfied led to the collapse.

- Adultery
- Unreasonable behaviour
  such as drink, drugs, gambling, violence, extravagance, meanness, neglect, refusing to have sex or to have children, excessive sexual demands, mental instability, homosexuality, persistent nagging
- Two-year desertion
- Two-year separation with consent from the respondent
- Five-year separation

Adultery

Many marriages survive some infidelity, but the infidelity may become grounds for divorce when your spouse has committed adultery and you find it intolerable to go on living together. You may be able to name the other person involved, but there is no necessity to do so. Some solicitors will advise you not to name the person, even when you know who it is, to save yourself embarrassment. However, more likely you will feel angry with your spouse, and one way of venting those feelings is to name the other person (the co-respondent).

There are occasions when a person believes that his or her spouse has been unfaithful – but cannot prove it and the spouse denies it. In these circumstances if the person wants a divorce he or she will have to cite some other grounds in the petition.

You cannot petition for divorce if *you* are the adulterer; there can be a divorce if you admit your liaison and your spouse chooses to use it as grounds on which to dissolve the marriage – you will therefore be the respondent (i.e. the recipient of the petition).

Remember, adultery can be cited as the grounds for divorce even if it takes place for the first time after you and your spouse have stopped living together.

Unreasonable behaviour

Citing unreasonable behaviour as grounds for divorce can be tricky. You have to prove that your spouse's behaviour is so unreasonable that it is impossible for you to continue to live together.

As the list above shows, there are some clear-cut examples of unreasonable behaviour over which there will be little argument, but there are many more examples which are rather grey and open to question. And remember, what is quite acceptable behaviour for one husband or wife may be completely intolerable for another.

One risk of citing unreasonable behaviour is that when you list the faults of your wife, say, that have driven you crazy there is a strong likelihood that she will see that as hostile, retaliate and list your bad habits, and explain why your demands drove her to behave in the way she did. None of us likes to see our shortcomings spelled out, so many solicitors recommend that their clients avoid proving these grounds if there is an alternative.

What is often odd about the citation of unreasonable behaviour is that it may have been tolerated for years by a husband or wife who then over a period of months finds it increasingly irritating and then impossible. A woman's obsessive cleanliness may start as a joke in the early years of a marriage and then turn sour as the obsession leads to inflexibility.

Drink, sex and violence

Heavy drinking is one of the most common examples of unreasonable behaviour. A wife could argue that her husband's drinking changed his personality so much that he was no longer the man she married.

Mary, who had two young children, found her husband's sexual demands too much: he wanted intercourse every night, and if he had to go away on a business trip he expected to be able to make up the lost opportunities on his return.

Violent behaviour is not infrequently cited, but the divorce court will not penalize a violent individual financially any more than an adulterer or a gambler. If a battered wife wants her husband to be convicted she must go to the police and make them charge him with assault.

Extravagance

Many people going through a divorce worry that their particular habits may be used as a weapon against them, so that when it comes to making financial arrangements they will be penalized.

For example, a wife (who would not keep the house clean and tidy, even though she did not work outside the home) might worry that she would be financially penalized for this behaviour. She only has to worry if she ran up huge food bills and spent thousands of pounds a year on clothes, and this reckless spending was central to her husband's claims of her unreasonable behaviour.

Neglect

There are no absolutes in unreasonable behaviour. What one husband finds intolerable from his wife (say, her disappearing at short notice with the children to visit her parents) may form the basis of another's stable marriage because the second husband values the time on his own. This is a classic example of the difficulties of interpretation which can be encountered when unreasonable behaviour is cited.

It was successfully cited when a wife objected that her husband wanted them to spend every Sunday with his parents, rather than spend time with her. From that example, proving that one party was devoting less and less time to the marriage and more and more time to work or to a hobby (whether it is football or hunting) could be a relatively neutral way of expressing unreasonable behaviour.

Pitfalls of citing unreasonable behaviour

As we have already mentioned, unreasonable behaviour is often a question of interpretation, and people citing it in the petition may be surprised to find their grounds rejected.

Ruth, 32, said that the main reason for divorce was because she wanted children and her husband Paul, who was slightly younger, did not. This was not sufficient grounds by itself, so her solicitor advised her to pad out the details. Ruth said that Paul was immature, spent all his time partying and really did not want to be married at all.

When Paul received the petition he accepted most of the details, although he objected strongly to the claim that he did not want to have children.

Another husband was so incensed by a relatively tame unreasonable behaviour petition that he did not bother to reply, but slammed in his own adultery petition. With such an acrimonious beginning, this divorce had little chance of being amicable. Had the husband's solicitor been more conciliatory there should have been some attempt made to dissuade him from submitting the adultery petition.

When unreasonable behaviour is to be used, a good solicitor will have the courtesy to warn your spouse's solicitors in advance about what is likely to appear on the petition so that reasons for the breakdown of the marriage can be amended and accepted by both sides and couched in the most gentle terms. This also speeds up proceedings.

Leaving out some grisly details to spare your spouse will not reduce your chances of a fair settlement – divorce proceedings and financial proceedings are separate issues. The details only have to satisfy the district judge that there are sufficient grounds to enable him or her to grant a certificate for divorce, although if the grounds are too tame some district judges will say that there are insufficient grounds for divorce.

Two-year desertion
Your spouse has deserted you for a continuous period of two years or more.

Two-year separation
You and your spouse have been living separately for two years or more and your spouse agrees to the divorce.

Five-year separation
You and your spouse have been living separately for five years or more, whether or not your spouse consents to the divorce.

The last two grounds for divorce differ from the first three in that it can be argued that it is the nearest that current divorce law comes to a no-fault divorce. In the first three cases the respondent can be said to carry more of the responsibility for the breakdown of the marriage than the petitioner, although this will have little bearing on the financial arrangements, except in terms of who pays the costs.

In emotional terms both sides must share the responsibility for the breakdown of a marriage. Even when a wife commits adultery and her husband feels that he is the injured party, at some stage he should ask himself some searching questions, such as: 'What happened to us that made her want to go off with another man?'

PAPERWORK

Although divorces involve judges and courts, they are not places of retribution. Most of the legal exchanges between your solicitor, the court and your spouse's solicitor take place on paper. You may have to make an appearance before a judge to discuss the arrangements that have been made about your children, but otherwise it is only when there is a major disagreement that you and your spouse will have to appear in court, and then only at a county court or at the High Court.

Divorces are private matters, and the number of people who read your papers are select and will be limited to you and your solicitor, your spouse and his or her solicitor, the district judge who sees the petition and grants the decree nisi; and any other judge or registrar who has to adjudicate over the financial arrangements, who may not even read the petition but just the affidavits relating to the financial side of the divorce. All these people are sworn to secrecy.

Filing a petition

When a petition is filed, a junior solicitor will, literally, take a piece of paper (which may be a standard form, although some firms of solicitors produce their own version) with the details of the marriage from the petitioner's solicitors to the divorce registry – which is at Somerset House in The Strand, London. Any divorce filed in England and Wales can be filed there, but it is not the only place for this.

A petitioner's solicitor will usually choose the nearest registry for convenience – most county courts in England and Wales have a divorce registry attached. If both parties live in the Midlands, for example, even though one of them is using a firm of London solicitors, it makes sense for the divorce to be processed at the registry in Coventry.

Details that accompany the petition

When the petition is filed in the divorce registry, your solicitor will send some other forms outlining your financial needs and the possible arrangements for your children (see examples in Appendix B). You must provide your full names, the date and place of your marriage, the address at which you both last lived together and your present addresses, your occupations, and the full names of your children and their dates of birth if they are under 18. Any details of court proceedings relating to your marriage or your finances must be put in the petition. In addition, the grounds for the irretrievable breakdown of your marriage must be given.

'The prayer' comes at the end of the petition. This asks the court to end the marriage, asks the court to ratify the arrangements made for your children, asks that costs should be awarded against the respondent (in cases of adultery or unreasonably behaviour) or the co-respondent (in cases of adultery) and to ratify the financial arrangements you are likely to make for yourself and your children.

These details are often filled in without much thought and often without any discussion and, as a result, may cause unnecessary bitterness. As you will see in the next chapter most of this bad feeling can be avoided if you give detailed information to your solicitor at an early stage in the proceedings.

If you are the respondent or named co-respondent you will receive copies of the petition and the other forms from the divorce registry within a few days. Try not to lose your temper when you read them: the details may be wildly inaccurate, but do not immediately blame your vindictive spouse: the forms may well have been filled in perfunctorily by the solicitor.

Legally, you and your spouse can continue to live together for up to six months after the grounds cited in the petition, say, adultery, occurred, to allow for reconciliation. However, if you are still living together six months after the last incident of adultery, it is argued that the infidelity was not as destructive as suggested in the petition, and the divorce will not be granted.

There is a little more leeway in terms of time for reconciliation as far as unreasonable behaviour is concerned, but your spouse's behaviour may not be quite as unreasonable as you have declared if you are still living together after six or seven months. And after a two-year separation is filed as grounds for divorce, should you attempt a reconciliation that fails after a couple of months, you must wait for two years, three months and one day before filing the petition.

Acknowledgement
Within eight days of receiving the copy of the petition, the respondent must acknowledge it by returning another form, called the 'acknowledgement of service', to the court. The respondent must indicate whether or not the divorce is to be defended, whether he or she will dispute the claims for costs made in the petition, and what claims will be made about children.

Once the respondent and co-respondent (in cases where adultery is cited) have returned their acknowledgement of service forms, the court sends copies to the petitioner.

Undefended divorces
The vast majority of divorces are undefended. When there are no wrangles about money or care of the children, an undefended divorce can proceed swiftly and relatively cheaply.

Defended divorces
Defended (or contested) divorces are rare nowadays and are seldom recommended. They end up in open court, the press and public are allowed to be present, they are expensive and acrimonious and the only winners are lawyers. They are also absurd. If one's spouse wants a divorce that badly, there would seem to be very little point in trying to stop him or her, and nothing of any emotional worth left with which to salvage the marriage.

A respondent determined to defend a divorce must send the 'answer' to the court within 29 days of receiving the copy of the petition, although extra time is given if the documents have to be sent abroad. The answer has to give every detail of why the divorce should not go ahead.

Applying for decree nisi and preparing the affidavit
If no answer has been filed/the divorce is not defended, the petitioner can now apply for decree nisi to be pronounced by the divorce registrar. The most serious stage of the proceedings now starts.

The petitioner's solicitor prepares an affidavit for the petitioner to swear confirming that the contents of the petition are true (some details may have been amended after discussions with the respondent's solicitors), including details about the arrangements for children. If there are any question marks over the arrangements, they will be clarified during the Section 41 appointment when parents will be asked to appear in court – usually on the same day decree nisi is granted. You must be scrupulously honest when the affidavit is drafted. Flamboyant exaggeration in the affidavit will be frowned on by the district judge.

The affidavit will include details such as where husband and wife have been living since the last bout of drinking or gambling (if that is cited in the petition) or since the petitioner knew about the adultery. This is because time limits apply to prevent old incidents being dredged up which the respondent could reasonably expect to be forgotten.

The affidavit will then be filed at the court with a request for decree nisi to be pronounced under the 'special procedure' – another piece of paper. A district judge looks through these papers and, if they seem in order, gives a certificate for decree nisi to be pronounced.

The petitioner and respondent will then be told the date fixed for decree nisi, usually four to six weeks later, although they may not know the date until the week before. Precisely when the parties are told and how quickly the date is fixed depends on the efficiency of the court.

If the agreement about the arrangements for the children has been reached between the parties, the judge is unlikely to interfere with that agreement.

If agreement has not been reached, the judge may ask the parties (accompanied by their solicitors) to attend an informal appointment to explore a solution to the difficulties. If a solution cannot be reached readily, this will delay the application for the final divorce decree.

Applying for decree absolute
Six weeks and one day after the date that decree nisi is granted, the petitioner's solicitor can apply for the decree to be made absolute. This again is done by paper – a form is sent to the court. The decree may be processed within 24 hours, longer if the court has to deal with a great many cases at the time.

Three months after that, if the petitioner has not already applied for decree absolute, the respondent may do so and the marriage is finally over, provided the petitioner does not object, or that if he or she should the objection is not upheld by the court.

If the petitioner continues not to agree for 12 months after decree nisi was declared because of financial wrangling, the petitioner's solicitors will have to explain to the registrar the reason for the delay and more specifically confirm in writing that the parties have not cohabited during the period or given birth to any children.

However, wrangles over money may continue for months and years. When complicated arrangements have to be made the financial proceedings may go on, literally, for years.

A good example of this is the arrangement between Herbert and Angela. They were divorced in 1981, but their financial affairs were still in the hands of their solicitors in 1988 and not finally sorted out until 1990. Herbert ran a business, and there were continual disputes about the value of the business and the size of the lump sum settlement that Angela would accept. It was an emotional disaster for both parties.

DECREE NISI
The terms *decree nisi* and *decree absolute* as used in the divorce process can seem mysterious. Those with a smattering of Latin will realize that *nisi* means 'unless'. But unless what? The answer is, *unless* there are reasons why the divorce should not be made absolute, such as for example the couple having not lived apart for two years as stated in the petition.

It is possible to back out of the divorce after decree nisi is granted and ask for the decree nisi to be revoked provided both petitioner and respondent agree, stay married, and pay hefty legal fees. You are married until decree absolute is granted.

Table 1 : Flow Chart of Divorce Proceedure

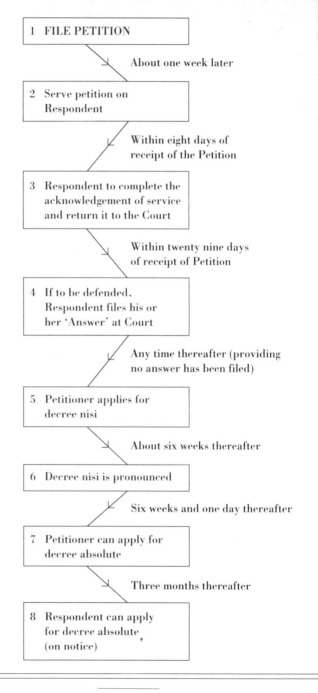

1 FILE PETITION

About one week later

2 Serve petition on
   Respondent

Within eight days of
receipt of the Petition

3 Respondent to complete the
   acknowledgement of service
   and return it to the Court

Within twenty nine days
of receipt of Petition

4 If to be defended,
   Respondent files his or
   her 'Answer' at Court

Any time thereafter (providing
no answer has been filed)

5 Petitioner applies for
   decree nisi

About six weeks thereafter

6 Decree nisi is pronounced

Six weeks and one day thereafter

7 Petitioner can apply for
   decree absolute

Three months thereafter

8 Respondent can apply
   for decree absolute
   (on notice)

*H*OW TO HELP YOUR SOLICITOR

Visiting a solicitor's office for the first time can be a traumatic experience. When you married, however many years before, it was the last place you imagined you would find yourself; and becoming another divorce statistic, while you know the process is such an intensely personal event, will only add to your feelings of dread.

You may find it easier to deal with all your conflicting emotions by concentrating on the practicalities of the divorce. If you can organize your affairs yourself you will save yourself a great deal of anxiety, keep your costs down and help your solicitor.

The more information you give your solicitor at the beginning of proceedings the better. You may feel inclined to conceal the details of all your assets on the grounds that you may end up with a better deal in the end. This is madness: there is a strong possibility that you will be forced to disclose everything anyway.

Moreover, if you attempt to conceal details and the judge suspects that is what you have done, he or she may penalize you on suspicion alone. Come clean from the beginning and you will have the fairest deal – however greedy you may think your spouse is. However, if you genuinely believe that your spouse is being excessively demanding, be prepared to fight it out in court, in which case the best way to obtain the fairest deal – for both sides – is to provide sound evidence of your previous needs and/or income and assets.

INFORMATION YOU NEED TO SUPPLY

Here is a checklist of the information that your solicitor will require. The more you can provide, the quicker and easier it will be to sort out your financial affairs. This list is not comprehensive and the details will depend on your and your partner's financial circumstances. Some information may be rather difficult to obtain, particularly if you are not on speaking terms with your spouse, but if you have suspicions about hidden assets the court can demand that they be disclosed.

General details
- Your full names and those of your spouse, and your dates of birth.
- Date and place of marriage, and a copy of the marriage certificate. If you cannot find it or only have a photocopy it is worth obtaining a certified copy immediately, because one will be needed when divorce proceedings start. You can either go yourself or write to the General Register Office (address given in Appendix C) for a copy. If you go yourself it costs £5.50 and will be sent to you after four working days. If you write it costs £15.00 and takes four weeks (costs and length of time as of March 1992). Alternatively, ask the superintendent registrar in the district in which you were married, or the clergyman at the church where you were married.
- Dates of any previous marriage(s) (for yourself and/or your spouse), and date(s) of decree(s) absolute.
- Copies of any court orders relating to this marriage or any previous marriages.
- Names and ages of children – including children from a previous marriage/relationship living in the matrimonial home.
- Your address and your spouse's if you are no longer living together. Addresses of any properties you and your spouse own – whether or not they are in both your names.
- Your home and work telephone numbers.
- Your occupation and that of your spouse.
- Names and addresses of your children's schools.
- Name, address and telephone number of your spouse's solicitor, and any correspondence you have received from that solicitor.

Financial details
It is a good idea at this stage to give a summary of your financial position:

- Your income and that of your spouse (if you know it).
- Details of your property: its approximate value, the size of your mortgage and the name and address of the mortgage lender and the account number.
- Copies of your bank statements and building society account details. Ask your solicitor how many years you should cover, but the most

recent two should be a sufficient guide to your incomings and outgoings. However, if your fortunes have changed dramatically in recent months and this is unlikely to be a permanent change (i.e. a business has collapsed or you have come into a large sum of money), find copies of statements that give a more realistic reflection of your typical financial affairs.

You should include details of all accounts held offshore or abroad. You may not think your spouse knows of their existence, but can you be 100 per cent sure?

Other assets: give your solicitor details of your share portfolio, and of any monies held in trust for you or your children.

Do you have assets that cannot be realized because they belong to your family? – land, say, or a collection of porcelain or Hockneys? – they must all be mentioned. Is your fortune tied up in a family company? This will be discussed in Chapter 12. Do not be tempted to conceal any item – it is likely to haunt the proceedings, whether or not you do so deliberately.

You must also mention the pension arrangements made for you and your spouse – this, as we will show in Chapter 11, can have particular consequences when both parties are in late middle age.

Details of any debts or liabilities you have. For example, include details of credit cards not paid off, and of amounts outstanding on loans for cars or household improvements.

Details of expenditure

Draw up a budget of your monthly and annual expenditure. Indicate what you have paid yourself and what has been paid on your behalf:

- Community charge or its equivalent
- Mortgage (including details of life assurance if it is an endowment mortgage; house insurance, etc.)
- Gas, electricity and water bills
- Housekeeping
- Clothes for yourself
- Clothes for your children
- Costs for running a car and other travel costs
- Insurance, medical and dental bills for you and your children

- Miscellaneous items such as money spent at the hairdresser's/barber's, newsagent's, launderette, dry cleaners, etc.
- Entertainment – theatre/films/restaurants/weekend trips
- Holidays
- School fees
- Additional costs for children – entertainment, extra activities, etc.

The importance of these details will be discussed further in Chapters 8 and 10.

For wives (both with and without children) it is worth trying to do a similar exercise for the future. What monthly and annual budget will you need once you (and possibly the children) have left the family home and are living in a new house? Where can you expect to live (realistically)? A judge would never support your wish to move to a much more expensive area, although the judge may accept that you should continue to live in the same area if your children's schooling depends on it, or a move to a similar size house in a less smart area. Ring up a few estate agents in the area of your choice and find out the cost of suitable accommodation.

It is really worth while being well-organized from the beginning of divorce proceedings. Keep all your correspondence and documents safe, and keep copies of letters and details that you send your solicitor. The main advantage of giving your solicitor all this information is that it cuts down on the amount of time he or she has to spend on your case and means that it can be dealt with efficiently. Time means money in a divorce, and while you may not have to pay the costs yourself, the money will eventually have to come out of the family pool.

7
WHAT MAY HAPPEN DURING DIVORCE PROCEEDINGS

In an ideal world, once you and your spouse have decided that divorce is inevitable, you sort out your financial affairs amicably, decide how you are going to look after your children, where you are going to live, and then ask a solicitor to help with the paperwork and check that your arrangements are reasonable.

In the real world, a large proportion of couples cannot discuss these things at all without a furious and tearful argument developing. Some spouses often feel so bitter that they become obstructive, and behave so irrationally that it is impossible to talk to them.

Brian had left Hannah and two sons, aged 11 and 9, for another woman. Hannah was so enraged that for the first month she would not speak to him on the phone, and intercepted all his calls to the children. After six weeks Brian longed to see his children, but Hannah said that they hated him and did not want to see him.

Brian decided against seeing a solicitor at that stage because he was worried about the cost. He also felt so guilty that he was prepared to accept that his sons did not want to see him, and was reluctant to turn up and take them out of the blue. His decision was a mistake and a false economy, because it took a long time for him to regain their confidence. They believed that he had deserted them – not just their mother. A speedy legal intervention would have cost little – compared with the emotional cost – since Brian would have been granted an interim access order by the court, whatever Hannah might have wished.

As we explain in this chapter, when you are concerned about the way your spouse is behaving or you do not trust him or her, you must ask your solicitor for advice and possibly consider legal action before it is too late. The orders we outline are only relevant for England and Wales, but similar systems are followed in Northern Ireland and Scotland. We also look at separation as an alternative to divorce, and how to stop divorce proceedings if you and your spouse want a reconciliation.

41

FINANCIAL ARRANGEMENTS

Maintenance pending suit
During divorce proceedings, judges like the status quo to be kept, so if the husband has been paying the mortgage and bills this arrangement should continue, irrespective of where he is living. If he is also paying rent for a flat this will be a great incentive for him to make sure things are settled quickly.

If he is reluctant to continue paying the bills, his wife can apply for financial relief once the petition has been lodged. She is likely to be granted 'maintenance pending suit', which will give her some temporary income until long-term arrangements are settled and the decree absolute is granted. She can also apply for 'interim periodical payments' on behalf of her children.

Both of these applications, which must be backed up by detailed disclosure of the family's needs, can take over six weeks for a district judge to grant: the order can be back-dated, however, to the date of the application; therefore it is sensible not to delay. They usually only cover the applicant's day-to-day needs. The husband will normally file his own affidavit, setting out his financial circumstances.

These applications are also a way of forcing a reluctant husband to disclose his means, because in the absence of evidence a district judge is likely to take the most favourable view of his financial circumstances and make a generous order in the wife's favour.

Freezing assets
If you know that your spouse has considerable assets in his or her name and is likely to try to dispose of them before you touch them and you have evidence of this, you can freeze the assets (in England and Wales). While it will be difficult for you to obtain accurate details, it will help your application if you can name the assets you think exist and the banks that your spouse uses, so that the injunction can be served on the right places. If appropriate, banks can be ordered to attend a hearing with evidence of a person's accounts. You may attempt to obtain an injunction on your own, but most people will find a solicitor's advice invaluable.

Charge on property
When the matrimonial home is in your spouse's name only and you are concerned that your spouse might try to sell the house without telling

you, you can block any potential sale quite simply. If, for example, your spouse transfers the house to a foreign company, divesting him- or herself of any interest in it less than three years before your application to the court to set it aside, it may be assumed that he or she has been trying to defraud you. While your spouse would always be caught out (because you would be able to see from the records when the house changed hands), there may be little in practice that you can do if the money has already been spent or if your spouse has taken it abroad.

You can prevent this happening before or during the proceedings by applying for a charge in respect of the property (whether it is registered or unregistered land). When potential buyers check the records they would come across the charge, and would not go ahead until it was lifted – it is a black mark against the house, establishing your right of occupation as a spouse.

Many women feel that their husbands would be rather upset by this move, but the husbands in question will only learn about the charge if they try to sell or re-mortgage the house without their wives' agreement. Registering the charge against registered property involves filling in some forms and telling the Land Registry that you are the spouse in occupation. This charge also stops your spouse re-mortgaging the house. For example, had the house been in your husband's name only, he might have been tempted to raise money on the house by claiming it was owned by his company. He could not raise a loan on it if the land charge was in place, because his bank or building society would not want to risk their further advance being prejudiced by your prior charge.

A wife's land charge 'dies' as soon as you apply for decree absolute because the house ceases to be a 'matrimonial home', thus an alternative charge has to be put on the house pending agreement or order to protect the interest. A solicitor acting for a wife, for example, would not advise her to seek decree absolute until she was sure she would receive her share of the capital in the property or had protected her interest by some other method.

Section 30 of the Law of Property Act

When a spouse refuses to leave the matrimonial home, will not put it on the market or agree to a divorce, a court can order the house to be sold – under Section 30 of the Law of Property Act. This usually prompts the spouse to co-operate, because if the house is sold in this way he or she will only receive the proceeds to which he or she is strictly entitled legally (i.e. the amount he or she has invested in the property). In the case of a woman, if she instead goes through with proper divorce proceedings, she will most likely receive a larger share.

Other financial considerations

Credit cards

When a woman has access to her husband's credit cards, there may be trouble. Anthea was so distraught when Charles left her that she went on a massive spending spree. She tore off the details of purchases on the credit card statement and just sent him a note of the vast balance to pay. Charles wanted to cancel all the cards instantly, but this proved more difficult than he had imagined.

The arrangement they had was not unusual, with a husband paying off the couple's joint credit cards each month. If Charles cancelled the cards Anthea would have had little income, and they would have had to pay unnecessary legal costs as they sorted out interim maintenance. Charles instead agreed to pay Anthea in cash the average amount that she had spent on the cards over the previous six months, before cancelling the cards. This gave her some income but not unlimited credit.

Normal spending patterns

Wives should take care that their husbands do not try to reduce their normal spending pattern through meanness, provided they know their husbands can afford it. If you become too thrifty a housekeeper you will find it difficult to demand much higher maintenance when you have been able to live quite reasonably during divorce proceedings on a relatively modest sum. If your husband is not generous, and you find yourself running into difficulties, you should go to your bank manager to arrange a loan, explaining that it will be paid back when the financial settlement is made.

Wives will know when their husbands are playing games and when they genuinely cannot give as much money as they could before. The normal scenario is that a husband may have to support himself in rented accommodation and can no longer afford to pay his wife the same amount of housekeeping money. In these circumstances both sides have to trim their cloth.

A sensible wife will keep a detailed budget of what she spends when she is living on her own for the first time; her husband will then have no grounds for complaint, and will have to give his wife enough money to meet her reasonable needs.

Some couples find it impossible to behave in a civilized fashion, and make life unnecessarily miserable. While George and Jill were in the throes of divorce, he agreed to pay all the food bills at the end of each month for her and their two children – but not without petty point-scoring. He went through the supermarket till receipts item by item and deleted those he classed as 'unnecessary', deducting their cost from the sum he was prepared to reimburse.

The tensions that are unavoidable during divorce are exacerbated in a recession when it is difficult to sell houses and families are forced to stay together. Clearly this makes the trauma of divorce much worse, but the family must soldier on until the house is sold.

OTHER INTERIM ORDERS

Violence

Violent behaviour or severe mental cruelty is not uncommon in divorce. It may not be sufficiently serious to warrant police intervention and to bring charges or cause a mental breakdown, but it can still be unpleasant enough to make living together difficult, before or after the petition has been filed. Some men would be horrified if their wives started to throw plates; some women put up with degrading beatings.

Sally and Richard were comfortably off, but he was a bully. She was beaten once within the first three months of their marriage, and Richard continued to be difficult and threatening through four years of marriage and two children – striking her occasionally. Then something snapped and she could take the threats no longer. She found it difficult to admit to her solicitor what had happened, as she was so ashamed for herself and for Richard, but she agreed to file a petition on the grounds of his unreasonable behaviour. Yet there was a problem: Richard had nowhere else to go and Sally was concerned that he would become violent again.

Sally was granted an injunction which prevented Richard from molesting her. She also wanted to change the locks instantly, but as Richard and she were both co-owners of the property it was not possible to ban him from the matrimonial home. If Richard had then breached that initial injunction, Sally could then apply for another injunction to get him out of the house. Not unexpectedly, Richard started to behave better when the first injunction was granted. (In Scotland these orders are called *interdicts*). If the violence had been sufficiently serious, an order could have been made to get him out of the house.

SEPARATION WITHOUT DIVORCE

A minority of couples choose to separate and not to divorce, either for religious reasons, for the sake of the children, or for financial reasons (for example your husband has large pension provisions which are only payable to his widow). Nevertheless, as the couple will in fact be living apart they still need to have their financial affairs sorted out. There is no convincing evidence that such an arrangement will be better for the children. What makes the difference is whether you and your spouse are living together, not the public perception of what has happened, or what divorce signifies to you. Once you are separated the only thing that you cannot do is remarry, but as far as financial arrangements and arrangements for the children are concerned, you might as well be divorced.

If you do not want to divorce you may draw up either a separation deed or obtain a decree of judicial separation. Both are popularly called 'legal separation'. The former is a separation agreement which is simply an agreement – an arrangement which is mutually acceptable. The latter is a formal legal status, which results in a decree of judicial separation, and the courts' powers can be invoked. In both cases the parties remain married.

Wealthy couples find separation easier, so far as the material aspects are concerned, particularly if they own a number of properties. William and Charlotte had a house in Chelsea and a house in Cambridgeshire. She lived in the country with the children, he claimed he needed to live in London for his work and spent many weekends abroad. Only their close friends realized, after they had not been seen together for over a year, that they were no longer living together. This arrangement went on for five years, until Charlotte wanted to remarry.

You should be aware that even though you have separated you are still married and, therefore, one or both of you may commit adultery. You may only realize what you have done when your spouse files the petition. Most solicitors will advise couples in this situation to divorce if the marriage has irretrievably broken down. This provides a degree of finality (even if the wife receives maintenance), giving both spouses the chance to rebuild their lives.

One of the disadvantages of a separation deed is that, unlike divorce proceedings, either side can ask for the terms of the agreement to be changed when the divorce actually occurs, if either of their financial circumstances has altered radically since the agreement was made. Most people want to know where they stand: this is the amount I have, or this is the amount I have to pay – and that is that – and not have to worry that two years later the negotiations start again. In addition, when you are simply separating you do not have the investigating powers of the court that exist if you are divorcing.

A separation deed always needs agreement. There are no sanctions if your spouse is dishonest. A court will rarely intervene over a deed of separation, because parties have entered into it voluntarily and with independent legal advice: they made their bed, they have to lie in it.

When there is a chance of a reconciliation, or there are no real grounds for the marriage to be dissolved (no adultery, unreasonable behaviour, or two or five years' separation), or there are huge pension rights involved and neither party wants to remarry, a separation deed or a decree of judicial separation may be the only answer. We discuss pensions in more detail in Chapter 11.

Before the financial order is made

Occasionally before the financial order is made, confirming the terms of the separation deed, the court may vary an agreement. Francesca, for example, who had a good salary as a personnel manager, suddenly developed multiple sclerosis and became seriously incapacitated. The court decided to impose maintenance on her former husband, Alan, although a clean break had been previously agreed in the separation deed.

RECONCILIATION

On the affidavit that follows the submission of a petition and that is filed in support of your application for decree nisi you have to declare whether or not you have continued to live under the same roof as your spouse. If your petition is based on adultery you are allowed six months (either continuously or as a total of shorter periods) from the last act of adultery in order to attempt reconciliation – if you exceed this period of time you will not be granted the decree on the grounds originally stated. Living under the same roof means not only cohabiting but existing as a couple. If, for financial or other reasons, it is impossible for one party to move out, make sure that no washing, cooking, cleaning or sharing of bedrooms is done in common after the reconciliation period is up.

When there is a late reconciliation, a couple should always try to stay married (you can get your divorce petition, and even your decree nisi, dismissed by consent). It is much simpler than divorcing and remarrying and is likely to be less expensive – in terms of legal fees – because the arrangements can simply be halted, and do not have to be formally undone.

You can apply to the court to dismiss your petition as soon as you think reconciliation is working. We discuss this further in Chapter 22. In Scotland, you can ask the court to stop proceedings for a reconciliation. If the reconciliation then does not work, you can pick up the proceedings from where you left off.

If you leave your application for the decree absolute for more than a year, you have to tell the court whether you have had a child since decree nisi, or whether you have continued to cohabit with your spouse since then, before the decree absolute will be granted.

APPEALS
The petitioner and the respondent can appeal against the court's decision in respect of a financial order or an order in respect of children. You should file a notice of appeal within five working days. You should ask for legal help in filing the notice because it will go from the district judge to the High Court, or from there to the Court of Appeal, and, in exceptional circumstances, on to the House of Lords. A decision to appeal should not be taken lightly – a higher court is unlikely to upset a lower court's order unless there is some error in law – the judge has a huge discretion and unless the result is manifestly unjust, the higher court will not interfere with the judgement. The process of an appeal is expensive, and unless it is successful the loser is likely to pick up both sides' legal costs.

8
ARRANGEMENTS WHEN THERE ARE NO CHILDREN

We have pointed out in Chapter 5 that sorting out a couple's financial affairs is a separate matter from the divorce proceedings. When there are no children there need not be any hitches, but if there are disagreements it will be over money, although the fighting does not have to end up in court, and rarely does so.

As far as legal procedure is concerned, the divorce proceedings activate the law which enables the court to make orders about dividing capital and income. In theory, the court has the power to give all the property of the husband to the wife (or vice versa), but the aim is to be fair to both parties and divide their assets so that at least their basic needs will be met.

In this chapter we shall consider the principles behind the arrangements made between men and women, when there are no children. But many of these still apply when there are children. We will look at:

- The old approach to dividing income
- The principle of need
- Short marriages and clean breaks:
  variations on the clean break
  when a clean break cannot be imposed
  marriages where there is a great age gap
  bitterness for men
  bitterness for women
- Long marriages:
  clean breaks v. maintenance
  a fully-entitled wife
  a semi-fully-entitled wife
  pensions
  bitterness

- Dividing assets:
  the matrimonial home
  other assets
- Choices for the very rich:
  clean breaks
  mixed arrangements

The law is governed by Section 25 of the Matrimonial Causes Act 1973, which sets out the range of factors which the court has to take into account when deciding how to deal with the assets of a divorcing couple. Those factors include the reasonable needs of the parties, their ages, earning capacities and assets – everything is put into the 'melting-pot'.

THE OLD APPROACH TO DIVIDING INCOMES

Until relatively recently 'a one-third' formula was applied: the husband's and wife's income would be added together and then divided by three. When one income was less than a third of the joint income, the spouse with the higher salary would have to make up the difference.

For example, Jim, aged 35, who was earning £45,000 p.a. in the City, separated from his wife Jane, who was earning £18,000 as a journalist. She was earning £3,000 less than a third of their joint income (£63,000), so she was able to argue that her share of their income should be enhanced.

This concept has fallen out of favour for a number of reasons, not least because it takes no account of the fact that three years later Jim might have lost his job while Jane could be earning £30,000 a year and be remarried. Nevertheless, the idea of adding both salaries together and dividing them roughly into three is often a starting point for negotiations.

THE PRINCIPLE OF NEED

Financial settlements are now based on need, and for a number of reasons women may seem to benefit more than men. Women still tend to be the lower earners, even when they have full-time careers, so their needs will be considered first.

For example, a wife will need somewhere to live, a car if she had access to one when she was married, money to pay off any outstanding debts on credit cards and enough to start afresh – almost as if the marriage had never taken place. When a couple has lived together for many years before they married this will be taken into account even if the actual marriage only lasted a couple of years.

The Matrimonial and Family Proceedings Act 1984 has set in motion a process whereby wives are encouraged to be more independent, and tries to move away from a situation where a husband has to maintain a young wife for the rest of her life.

There is now some expectation that a young or middle-aged wife and mother – after a reasonable period on her own – will develop a career of her own. However, when couples are over 50 the expectations for the wife will be lower.

So a wife, even when she has young children, will probably (only) be maintained until she is in her mid-forties, not until she is in her sixties or seventies. Many women think this unfair because a wife is never going to have the opportunity to establish a career in the way her husband has done if she looks after the children for 15 years.

Nevertheless, it is fairer than the practice which was common up until the 1960s, when husbands had to pay their wives maintenance for life, which was a terrible drain on their resources and often destroyed subsequent marriages.

SHORT MARRIAGES AND CLEAN BREAKS

The concept of the 'clean break' started to evolve through the 1970s, and it goes a long way to countering the drawbacks of maintenance.

What a clean break means is that the wife's maintenance payments are 'capitalized' – for example, a woman in her mid-fifties who after a long marriage might have expected maintenance payments of £15,000 a year, would be given a lump sum of, say, £200,000 on the basis that, if it were sensibly invested, it could give her the same sort of annual income for the rest of her life – although she would have to dip into the capital as she got older.

The 1984 Act gives courts the power to impose a clean break, if that is appropriate, although in practice a clean break will only be imposed in cases where there are either sufficient assets or there are no assets at all.

Clean breaks are most likely to affect people whose marriage has only lasted a few years, and where the couple is still young and both are working. A working woman in her late twenties or early thirties cannot expect any maintenance payments, as she is earning her own living and is capable of continuing to do so. A clean break will be arranged so that both parties receive a share of any capital they may have (which is usually tied up in a flat or house) – but if the husband earns a lot more than the wife she may receive a larger share of the capital in order to help set her up in a new home.

A clean break after a short marriage also makes sense emotionally. When a childless marriage ends there may be a great deal of sadness and bitterness, but men and women in their twenties and thirties have a good chance of marrying again. A clean break financially will help them make a clean break emotionally.

A woman who receives a cheque each month from her former husband is going to be reminded of that sadness and bitterness every time the envelope lands on her doormat or when she reads her bank statement. In addition, a clean break circumvents the problem faced by a woman and her children when her former husband defaults on his maintenance payments.

However, there may be circumstances when a man does not want a clean break because he does not really want a divorce and still loves his wife. He may find some consolation in sending her money each month until he is able to face the idea of life without her. Alternatively, he may suspect that she will remarry as quickly as possible (at which point maintenance automatically ceases) so it will make financial sense for him just to pay maintenance for a short time.

The clean break has the overriding advantage that neither party can apply to vary the order except in exceptional circumstances (for example fraud, duress or misrepresentation). This means that there is certainty for both parties and that if the payer does remarry eventually his or her new marriage is not haunted by the previous one and the payments which arose from it.

Variations on the clean break

A clean break sounds final, but there are a number of variations that indicate how agreements can be reached, bearing in mind the wife's needs. Michael and his wife Kathleen were both in their late twenties when they married. After a year, Michael's employers offered him a post in Hong Kong. Kathleen was a successful teacher (deputy headmistress of a primary school), but decided to go to Hong Kong and see if she could find a job there. After a couple of years they decided to separate – quite amicably. Kathleen came home but could not immediately find as good a job as the one she had had two years before. So Michael and his solicitor agreed that in addition to the lump sum settlement she should be given additional maintenance, for three years (term maintenance), while she re-established her career. As it happened, Michael was able to pay the money in one go; Kathleen's lump sum included an extra £15,000 for three years' maintenance (£5,000 a year). Kathleen could then decide whether she should invest it or live off it.

When a clean break cannot be imposed

When there are no assets, one spouse has a significantly higher income, and the husband and wife have been living in rented accommodation, clean breaks cannot always be imposed. Maintenance is likely to be paid on a monthly basis by the husband to the wife if he has a much higher salary, but he would not expect to have to pay that forever. The court could stipulate that maintenance would only be paid for, say, three years, after which time the wife would have no further call on her husband, no matter how their fortunes changed.

Marriages where there is a great age gap

Marriages between young women and older men (or vice versa) which last only a few years can lead to great bitterness. The young wife (and it is more frequently the case that younger women marry older men than the reverse) becomes used to a high standard of living and argues that she cannot be expected to drop to her previous standard of living, so demands a huge lump sum. The husband will argue that his wife had nothing before the marriage and that it was just her tough luck that the marriage did not work out. The wife might well get a lump sum if the case goes to court, however, so the husband might be well-advised to make her an offer, to try to prevent the costs and distress of a court hearing.

Bitterness for men

The guidelines applied to wives are not necessarily the same as those applied to husbands. In a short, childless marriage where the husband has sporadic earnings – say, as an actor – of about £12,000 a year, and his wife earns over £30,000 as a television producer, she would probably not be expected to pay either maintenance or an additional lump sum towards his living expenses when they divorce.

Her solicitors would argue that there was nothing that he had done to further her career (unlike Kathleen, who decided to go to Hong Kong to support Michael), and that he chose a career that he knew was risky and badly paid. It may be bad luck for him that his standard of living drops suddenly, but his reasonable needs are being met by what he earns on the boards.

Even if he argues that it was a joint agreement that he should have a go at acting for a few years and that if he failed he would change his career, it was still his choice to be able to do that. He was lucky to be married to someone whose earnings made a difference to their lifestyle.

Bitterness for women
Women suffer their fair share of bitterness after short marriages. A wife might realize that her husband's earnings are just beginning to take off, or that his business is beginning to gel at the time their marriage has come to an end – before she is able to benefit from the hard work that they have both put in.

A woman's future hopes cannot be recompensed, either. A woman in her mid-thirties who wants children will be deeply aggrieved if her husband leaves her for a younger woman, and may feel there is no time left for her to develop a new relationship and have children. All she can hope for – and clearly this will depend on the individual man – is that out of guilt he will agree to give her a larger share of the equity in the house than she might otherwise have expected.

LONG MARRIAGES
When a long marriage grinds to a halt and collapses, almost inevitably one side faces a bleak and lonely future. Long marriages which end truly though mutual consent are few and far between: usually the husband or wife meets someone else and decides that the prospects look rosier with this new partner.

When there are no children, or the children are no longer living at home, the spouse who has been left has to come to terms with rejection as well as the future. Many people who have been left in these circumstances say that they wish their spouse had died; they would only have to grieve for the loss of the person, not question how they had spent their adult life – had it really been a complete mockery?

For the vast majority of couples today, the husband will either have a higher salary or, if he is retired, have had the higher earning capacity. In future, because more women will have had careers, there will be much less disparity, and financial settlements will reflect this.

The financial settlements at the moment still depend, nevertheless, to a certain extent on whether or not the wife has worked or contributed substantially to the husband's financial success. Even when she has worked, if her husband is a high earner the wife may argue that she has supported him, oiled their social wheels and entertained his business associates for him. Her salary will be a small factor and be taken into account when reaching some agreement, but she will be entitled to a higher standard of living by virtue of her contribution than would a working woman with a high-earning husband whose marriage collapses after a few years.

Clean breaks v. maintenance

Ideally, all wives should hope for a clean break, with a lump sum to invest for income. In practice, there is rarely enough capital to house both husband and wife and provide a lump sum to be invested for her income. It is usual for the husband to pay his wife maintenance until she is self-sufficient; and either party can go back to court if he or she wants the sum to be reassessed.

Provided the wife does not remarry, she could in theory receive payments until her death. This is the unpleasant aspect of maintenance. A husband can never be certain that his obligations are over. In theory, a man in his later seventies may have been supporting his former wife for nearly thirty years, and every other year he has been asked to provide more money. As yet there are few such cases because divorce was relatively uncommon thirty years ago, but in the next few decades more and more divorcees will be around in their seventies and eighties.

If a husband maintaining his former wife dies without making reasonable provision for her in his will, the wife could make an application against his estate for the maintenance payments to be continued. It is therefore quite important for the husband to get advice on his will, to try to prevent any such application in the future.

Tax relief

One major change in taxation has changed the emphasis on maintenance. The 1988 Budget eliminated tax relief on maintenance payments; before that it was in the financial interest of many husbands to pay maintenance – particularly higher-rate tax payers and those who could not afford a lump sum settlement. Now a husband only receives the difference between a married person's and a single person's allowance in tax relief.

When there are sufficient assets, the court will decide whether a clean break or maintenance is the most suitable solution. A court, for example, could give a wealthy man a choice: either give your former wife £30,000 maintenance a year or a £250,000 settlement. The court can order what it thinks most fit.

In cases where older marriages fail, the husband's needs must not be overlooked. Valerie, aged 58, decided to leave her husband Edward, 62, after 30 years of marriage. She believed that she was entitled to an equal share of the capital, even though she was going to marry again. Edward argued, successfully, that he would need to employ a housekeeper to look after him for the rest of his life and Valerie therefore did not receive the lump sum she expected, as part of his capital was going to be tied up for that specific purpose.

Where there is a chance of remarriage after a long marriage, a husband will not want to pay his former wife an enormous sum of money in a clean break only to find that she remarries 18 months later. His wife, on the other hand, will want a clean break. How is the court likely to decide?

The court might order a clean break but would take into account the wife's intention to remarry. But in turn the wife might well argue: 'Well, yes, I do want to remarry, but my future husband is a struggling artist, hardly earns anything, and I still need to be rehoused and live on something, and that would be the case whether or not I remarried.' This can be devastating for a husband: not only does he lose his wife to another man, he has to provide a substantial sum for her.

A fully-entitled wife
A wife's ultimate claim comes when there has been a long marriage, and she is in her fifties or sixties; the children of the marriage have grown up and are no longer dependent on their parents and their

mother did not work at all during the marriage but chose to bring up the children. She is what is called 'a fully-entitled wife'. Her needs are the court's first consideration, bearing in mind her husband's means.

If a wife is in her forties and she married in her early twenties, there is an argument for saying she could find a job, although if she is not trained her earning capacity would be quite small. Husbands of wives up to their late forties often argue that the woman still has some earning capacity.

However, the chances are that these wives will still be entitled to a reasonable house and a reasonable standard of living because the court will recognize that they have made a huge contribution to the marriage in bringing up the children. Without any doubt both husband and wife will be worse off than if they had stayed married – the husband will have to support two households indefinitely.

A semi-fully-entitled wife

A 'semi-fully-entitled wife' has a small job, some private means or can expect some inheritance. This can cause real bitterness for the husband because the wife may demand money from him even though he knows that she comes from a wealthy family and can expect to inherit a considerable sum in due course, even though her parents are, say, in their seventies and hale and hearty.

The court will take limited notice of the long-term expectations of the wife – unless her parents are terminally ill. The wife's solicitor will argue that her parents may survive for another 20 years, they could change their wills or, alternatively, they could lose their fortune through poor investment.

Only when a husband knows that his wife will definitely receive money that is in a family trust might he successfully argue that this should be taken into account. The husband will probably opt to pay maintenance – which may be for some years – and then when he hears that, say, his former mother-in-law has died he will immediately make an application to the court for the maintenance to be stopped.

Pensions

For couples in their forties and older pension arrangements are crucial in the settlement, and because they are so complicated these will be discussed in detail in Chapter 11. Pensions are increasingly going to be a factor in a financial settlement because people now live much longer after retirement age.

Bitterness

It is human nature and quite understandable for a wife to hope to maintain her standard of living and not to see it drop after the divorce. Some wives argue that their husbands are not accepting a sufficient drop in their own standard of living compared with themselves and, of course, some husbands argue how greedy their wives are.

When the couple or the husband is rich, neither side will see any drop in their standard of living. But where there is an overall shortage of cash and capital, solicitors, and ultimately the court, have to decide by how much both parties will have to drop their standard of living.

Most bitterness is engendered when the husband is fairly certain that his wife is going to remarry. She may not have anyone in mind but he is convinced that there will be soon – she is an attractive, sociable person. He may feel that she deserves nothing, and even getting him to agree to 50 per cent of the capital in the former matrimonial home, which was in his sole name, can be an uphill battle.

DIVIDING ASSETS

The matrimonial home

When the house is in both names
An enormous amount of anger can be generated when it comes to splitting the major asset, usually the couple's home. If the property is in both names, irrespective of which of the two put most money in, the capital will, in theory, be divided in two.

For example, say a couple bought a house seven years ago for £160,000. They have a £40,000 mortgage and the wife put £100,000 towards the purchase, the husband £20,000. They will start off from the basis that they should each take half the capital out unless they spelled out in the deeds that the proceeds should be divided according to the contributions. Other factors will, however, also be taken into consideration: if the wife has other capital, is earning a good salary, and is easily able to buy another flat but her husband needs his half share of the capital to be able to buy himself a flat and has no other capital, it may be fairer that they have half the value of the house each regardless of the fact that she put much more money into it. If the wife has nothing but her interest in the house, the court may well decide to give her more than half to reflect her greater contribution.

Take another couple in a slightly different position. The wife's half share of the equity was £100,000 but she found somewhere to live in the country for £60,000. The husband's solicitors successfully argued that she had put only £15,000 towards the marital home, and had not paid any of the mortgage or the bills, and that because of these factors she was not fully entitled to £100,000. In this case she accepted £70,000.

When the house is in one name
Matters do become more complicated and acrimonious when a property is in only one name, often the husband's. The wife then has to show what she needs to be rehoused, and if the husband feels she has contributed little financially he will often feel embittered.

Section 17 of the Married Women's Property Act 1882/Section 30 of the Law of Property Act
There are circumstances where all the assets are tied up in the flat or house and the wife does not want a divorce and will not file a petition – even though the husband has left, wants to sell the house and marry someone else. The husband can apply to the court under Section 17 of the Married Women's Property Act 1882 or Section 30 of the Law of Property Act (entirely separate from the divorce legislation) to force the house to be sold.

In theory, when the property is in their joint names, the equity will be split in two, completely ignoring the wife's needs or the contributions made by either side to the marriage, and she will be forced to move. In practice, these applications rarely reach court because the reluctant spouse suddenly realizes the implications, and makes an application for a property adjustment order in divorce proceedings.

Too little equity
Even when a couple own their own flat or house, it may be worth too little to sell and re-house both husband and wife separately. In these circumstances, either the husband or the wife buys the other party out,

or they will have to sell the property, both live in rented accommodation and invest their share of the capital until their circumstances change and they are in a position to buy.

Other assets

In a short marriage when one or other of the parties have careers it is unlikely that they will be able to take further capital from their spouses because they will not have additional needs, after dealing with the house. Caroline and Philip both earn over £20,000 each. They are in their late twenties and their marriage has foundered after three years. Their standard of living has been much higher than might be suggested by their salaries because Philip has been the beneficiary of a number of trusts which give him sizeable chunks of money three or four times a year. Caroline wanted to benefit from that after the divorce, but Philip's solicitor successfully argued that her needs could be met out of the sale of their house and her own salary.

CHOICES FOR THE VERY RICH

Clean breaks

It is much easier to make financial arrangements if money is not an issue, and a clean break is nearly always arranged. You can understand why if you consider a couple who between them have two million pounds. They are unlikely to battle too much over money because there is enough to buy two substantial houses and there is sufficient income to keep both parties in champagne and smoked salmon.

If a man is worth, say, £10,000,000, the wife is unlikely to receive much more than, say, 10 per cent of his assets in excess of her housing needs unless, for example, she can show that without her his business would not have prospered. A few years ago the upper ceiling that a wife could expect would be £750,000 – it was considered that all her needs could be met with this sum. While that ceiling has now risen, even the wealthiest husbands are unlikely to have to part with much more than £2 million or in exceptional circumstances £5 million, if the wife has a particularly expensive interest. Such sums would enable a wife to buy a more than adequate house (and, for example, land if hunting had been her main interest), with the balance invested for income, and she would never have any financial worries.

Mixed arrangements

When the husband has a high income and considerable capital assets, the choices are, of course, greater. Alastair was well off in his own right, as well as earning a good salary as a broker. His wife Helen had been a successful cook before she married and was quite capable of earning a good living although she had worked less during their three years of marriage.

Helen argued for a lump sum settlement, but Alastair's solicitors said that he preferred to pay generous maintenance for three years while she built up her contacts again. Alastair's gamble paid off: Helen remarried within two years of the divorce, and at the point of remarriage Alastair's obligations ended.

Some wealthy husbands argue that instead of giving money to their former wives they would prefer to set up their children in their own flats; the money will, after all, be going to the children anyway, and the husbands argue that they cannot afford to do both. Unfortunately for these men, the court will not be happy about these suggestions: whatever the moral obligations towards his adult children, a man's legal obligation to his wife comes first, although any children who are still in full-time education are the court's overriding concern.

TAX ON MAINTENANCE AND TRANSFERS OF CAPITAL

Until the Budget in 1988, divorced men who were paying maintenance to their former wives and children could claim tax relief on the payments. This tax relief also covered school fees. Now, the government is much less generous so it is important that when a maintenance order is agreed, that both husband and wife understand the sums are net – the actual cost to the husband will be higher because he will have to pay the maintenance out of his net income, having already paid tax and national insurance contributions on it. He will continue, however, to be able to claim relief up to a maximum of the married person's allowance.

His former wife will not have to pay any tax or national insurance on her own maintenance payments or on the money she receives on behalf of her children – that will, obviously, have already been paid by her former husband.

Similar care must be taken to avoid any misunderstandings when there is a transfer of capital between one spouse and the other. The transfer of assets to a spouse might attract capital gains tax and it is important to bear that fact in mind when calculating the value of the assets.

There is however a Capital Gains Tax exemption which applies as between husband and wife who are living together. The effect of this is that spouses who have assets which are likely to be the subject of property adjustment orders or divorce (apart from the matrimonial home, which is dealt with by a separate exemption) and which are of sufficient value to attract a liability to capital gains tax would be well advised to attempt to deal with those assets prior to separation or in the year of assessment during which they last live together as husband and wife.

In this context it is also worth reading Chapter 12: a woman might expect that her husband will sell part of his business in order to give her a generous lump sum. She may be mistaken, if only because the sale might result in enormous capital gains payments, and so she should not be encouraged to spend a disproportionate amount of money having independent financial advisers assess the value of the company. If it is a family business and other members of the husband's extended family depend on it for their livelihood, the company is extremely unlikely to be sold, capital gains aside.

9

PRACTICAL ARRANGEMENTS FOR CHILDREN

Robert, a businessman in his early forties, was forced to admit to his solicitor that neither he nor his wife Susan wanted to look after their seven-year old son and five-year old daughter.

Susan had met a Canadian who spent a great deal of time travelling, and she wanted to be free to go with him. Robert had a demanding job and was honest enough to say that, while he was happy to be the children's father, he could not be their mother as well: he simply could not do the school run, take them to dancing classes and swimming, and arrange their dental appointments. He did not really want the divorce.

This bleak tale is a mercifully rare example of the depressing effect divorce can have on a family. Fortunately, it had a happy ending (of sorts). The couple divorced; the children went to live with Robert, who remarried within 18 months to a woman delighted to take responsibility for the children. Tragically for Susan, who is now based in London, although she is able to see her children regularly it would not be realistic for her to expect to have them living full-time with her again.

While making arrangements for the children can be straightforward, sadly there are many instances when the children are manipulated emotionally for their parents' ends. Good parents do their best not to turn their children against their former partners, but the temptation to influence the children is often overwhelming and, as a result, there may be protracted battles in court and many parents, usually fathers, ultimately lose contact with their children.

If a family ends up in court, the children's views are of course taken into account. Children over the age of 9 are interviewed by the court welfare officer. Orders cannot be made for children of 16 or over.

The next chapter looks at the financial arrangements that are made for children. This chapter will look at different aspects of the practical arrangements that can be made for looking after children:

- The language of the law: the legal terms used to describe post-divorce arrangements for children
  Making a voluntary agreement with your spouse
- What part the court plays
- Contact arrangements
- Education
- Court welfare officers
- Loss of and changes in residence arrangements

THE LANGUAGE OF THE LAW

Before we discuss the different practical arrangements that parents may make for their children, it is important to understand the legal terminology used to describe the position of divorcing parents. The law is now governed by the Children Act 1989, which came into effect on October 1, 1991, and which has made many significant changes to the law relating to children. This operates in parallel to Section 41 of the Matrimonial Causes Act 1973 (see Appendix A).

The key aspects of the new law can be summarized as follows:

- both parents following divorce retain what is known as 'parental responsibility', irrespective of the actual practical arrangements made for the children. This means that both parents, either jointly or independently, may take decisions about the child's upbringing. Obviously, where a child is living with the mother, the mother will take most day-to-day decisions; but wider questions, such as education and religious upbringing, may have to be decided jointly. The only limits on a parent's freedom of action are (i) that it must not conflict with a court order and (ii) that the other parent may, if he or she disagrees, go to court to challenge a decision. Thus, a parent who does not have the child living with him or her does *not* lose all legal status in respect of the child.
- separate from the issue of parental responsibility is the question of the practical arrangements for the children. The 1989 Act introduces new orders (under Section 8) to describe these:
  'residence' orders, which describe where and with whom the child is to live;
  'contact' orders, which describe those with whom the child is permitted to have contact, the forms of contact, and the conditions under which it is to take place; and

'specific issue' and 'prohibited steps' orders, which allow one parent to go to court to resolve a specific disagreement or to prevent the other parent from taking a particular step in relation to the child, for example, changing the child's school without agreement.

- an important new principle is that the courts will not always make a residence or contact order, but will only do so when they consider it to be in the child's interests. The most likely case in which orders will be made is where the parents disagree about practical arrangements. So, if the parents can agree, there will be no need for an order. As we have seen, both parents retain a legal status as a parent irrespective of whether the court makes an order or not.

- the practical arrangements being proposed for the children still have to be shown to the court, in some detail, but it is only in rare circumstances that the court will wish to make more detailed enquiries of its own, in which case a Section 41 appointment is fixed by the court. For the record, Section 8 of the Children Act can be invoked in many different situations and not just by the parents (unlike Section 41). For example, grandparents who fall out with their son and want to continue to see their grandchildren could apply for a contact order.

Thus, the law now provides a clear framework for describing parents' legal position while simultaneously reducing the need to invoke court procedures.

The parent with whom the children are living has everyday responsibility for the children. This parent is obliged to make sure that the children go to school on time, do their homework, are fed; he or she decides how much time they should spend watching television, supervises the time they spend with friends, and enforces bedtimes. The younger the children the more important it is for one parent to take prime responsibility.

Mothers usually have their children living with them, but in future, as men play a larger part in bringing up their children and women pursue careers, it is likely that more men will have children living with them. A working mother with a full-time job will not necessarily be the parent to provide the children with a home – the arrangements made in a particular family will be a reflection of the mores of the people involved.

Julian and Faith are both teachers; Faith has just been made deputy head of a large comprehensive. Quite voluntarily, she has suggested that their two teenage children should live with Julian. While some people may think that their decision is odd, they and their friends think it is eminently sensible, and Faith does not feel that this presents any kind of slur against her as a mother – she did more than her share of parenting when the children were small.

WHAT PART THE COURT PLAYS

You may think that your children will be better off not living with both their father and mother in an acrimonious atmosphere, but even if the advantages of not living as a family seem overwhelming, there will always be some disadvantages that will haunt you forever. You must recognize that divorce is a painful process for all involved, and both parents and children are going to feel some injustice and bitterness. It is up to solicitors and the court to minimize that sense of injustice.

When children are involved, it is best to come to some agreement with your spouse, because a judge might impose an arrangement that neither of you want (although this will only happen rarely). Remember also that any arrangement primarily must ensure that the children's physical and emotional needs will be met. Reach agreement if you can; and even if you feel the agreement is unsatisfactory you will still probably do much better by agreeing than by allowing the courts to decide for you.

Some parents recognize the consequences of their actions immediately and sort things out for their children amicably. If this can be done there will be no need even to seek a court order. The judge is only likely to enforce different arrangements if the life you and your spouse envisage for your children is constantly being disrupted, or if your plans are thought to be ridiculous.

When parents initially disagree, and after some struggle one side comes up with what it considers an obvious solution to the situation, the courts may not always agree. Your freedom of action becomes limited; you may not be able to take the children abroad suddenly without going back to court. This may lead to delays and frustrations, but you must always remember that the Law is hovering in the background.

After a shortish marriage, Marie-Anne decided to take her two young children to live in her native France. While the court was happy to let her do this, her former husband, Barry, objected on a number of grounds, including religion, because he did not want his children brought up as Catholics. The court finally agreed in favour of Marie-Anne, but Barry remains free to return to the court in due course if he can prove that his fears have some basis.

One spouse may make frequent appearances in court when he or she is carrying on a vendetta against the other party and, tragically, using the children as pawns. Other parents may also go to court regularly because they are unusually obsessive about one aspect of the way their children are being brought up. Such parents cannot come to terms with the fact that they have to relinquish that obsession because it is simply not practicable to exercise day-to-day control when the children are not living with them.

CONTACT ARRANGEMENTS

The courts rate children's stability highly and will not accept too many changes in their lives, but they also encourage both parents to keep in touch. One common pattern is for children to spend every other weekend with their father (if he is not the primary carer) and longer periods with him in the holidays.

A mother may try to argue that the children should not see their father as frequently because it is going to cause a lot of disruption to their lives. Their visits cause her despair, because her former husband appears regularly to pick them up and she wants to avoid the emotional hassle for herself that this contact entails. In this sort of circumstance, and if no agreement can be reached, the court will often grant the father greater contact than the mother wants or thinks is appropriate.

The sort of contact arrangements that will be granted depend on where the father is living, and what he can provide and do for the children. When he has a home to which he can take the children, the children may be allowed to stay with him much sooner than many mothers wish.

Young children

When the children are very young, the court may take more responsibility in deciding what the arrangements will be, in conjunction with court welfare officers – the 'social workers' employed to report on cases for the benefit of the court. This is one of the sadder consequences of a marriage breakdown.

The children may have to lose some of their independence, if the court decrees that they should not lose contact with their father, even if it means a 4-year-old has to spend the day with his father rather than go to a party.

The court can also make specific and seemingly petty orders. When husbands and wives cannot sort out the details sensibly, the court may intervene and order a 7 p.m. pick-up every other Friday, with a return at 7 p.m. on the Sunday. Of course, when these orders are imposed rigidly they will be resented even more.

Allowing children to stay with their father for short periods is, of course, more difficult when children are small. Some fathers do not always recognize that young children may feel insecure when they are taken away from their mothers and familiar surroundings to stay at a strange place, so the children's age is a consideration. When the mother has some help, the nanny or mother's help may be asked to go with the children to provide some support and continuity. Nevertheless, children are expected to be quite robust emotionally by the time they are six or seven.

Contact can cause severe emotional problems for a mother of young children whose feelings for them may become a substitute for the relationship with her former husband. Her resentment may be even greater when her husband is living with another woman who she thinks has taken her husband away. The mother simply does not want her children to go and stay with their father and another woman.

This works both ways: fathers, too, often have to live with the idea of their children being looked after by their mother's new husband – for most of the time – and the feelings of bitterness and resentment this causes can last for years.

Older children

Children will tend to stay together and will not be split up unless they are very much older and make the decision themselves, for example, daughters choosing to stay with their mother and sons with their father. Having said that, if one son is very difficult to cope with, he might go and live with his father, or when there is a big difference in age of the siblings, a teenage boy might go and live with his father while his five-year-old brother stays with their mother because there is no real necessity to keep them together. However, these sort of arrangements are not common.

Older children, quite naturally, will want to stay near their friends so they can maintain their social life and interests. It does not really matter which parent's house they live in, continuity of their own life is much more important. It will be self-defeating for a father to insist that an older child visits him if the child resents the disruption to his own plans.

Up until the age of 18 a parent can go to court on a child's behalf if the child is not happy with the arrangements.

Children over the age of 18
Once the children are 18 a father cannot be compelled by law to provide somewhere for them to live although, in practice, especially if the child is in full-time education, one parent will provide some base.

Novel arrangements
Some couples manage to have novel arrangements that enable both of them to keep in close touch with their children. Sam and Rowena lived in a large Georgian house which they converted into two flats when they divorced. Sam lived on the ground floor, Rowena on the top floor, and their two children in the middle.

When Sam remarried, he and his second wife managed to buy the house next door – they sold their original flat and part of their new house to finance the arrangement. Their two children were still able to see both parents every day, and while this arrangement would not suit all couples it worked for this particular family.

The position of grandparents and other relatives
There may be times when a grandparent (or other relative) wishes to have some formal legal status with respect to the child. This is most likely to be the case where the parents and grandparents have fallen out either before or after the parents' divroce.

The Children Act 1989 improves the position of relatives in this respect. Under the Act, a relative can apply for a residence or contact order if the child has been living with that relative for at least three years. A relative may also apply for residence or contact if (as seems unlikely if there is a dispute) both parents consent. Alternatively, if a residence order is already in force with respect to the child (for example, in favour of the mother following a divorce of the parents) then a relative may seek one of these orders if the parent in whose favour the residence order was made consents to the application. Otherwise, a relative will have to seek leave of the court before making an application for residence or contact.

EDUCATION
Even when parents are bitterly arguing about money and their possessions, they may be in total agreement over what type of school their children should attend.

Occasionally, however, one parent will go to court to argue about whether a child should go to boarding school or not, and often this has little to do with the cost. Some fathers want their children to go away to school because it will break the tie with their mother and the fathers believe that this will diminish her influence over the children.

Peter's 14-year-old son, Matthew, was unruly. Peter believed that his behaviour at home would be sorted out by a school where there would be more discipline. He blamed his former wife Margaret, who he believed was rather weak. In truth, he was envious of her relationship with Matthew and hoped that boarding school would reduce her 'hold over the boy'.

Margaret wanted Matthew at home and was concerned that she would lose touch with him, and also believed that boarding education was not suitable for him. She argued that Peter's expectations of the 14-year-old were far too high, while she also admitted that one parent was unlikely to be unable to discipline the child as effectively as two parents. She was concerned that Matthew would feel even more rejected if he were sent away to school. The court would of course take Matthew's own views into account. If there had been a tradition of public school education in Peter's family it would have been more likely that his wishes would have been granted.

The court, in fact, sympathized with Margaret because she clearly had a better understanding of how Matthew was going to react. She went to court and described the options from Matthew's point of view – and the court followed her lead.

Sometimes a compromise will be struck over the age at which child is sent to boarding school. A rather unusual case concerns the eight-year-old son of a peer, who will eventually inherit the title. His father wants the child to go to boarding prep school even though he himself hated it. The father believes that a public school education will give his son the best chance of coping with the sort of lifestyle he inevitably will have to adopt. The courts were sympathetic towards the mother, who did not want her son to go away at eight because he was too young. But at 11, with public school looming at 13, there were fewer grounds for dissent.

There are rare cases where the parents might not have discussed education at all, say, when the children were under four at the time of the divorce and arguments only develop when the children reach the ages of nine or ten. A lot of people who can afford it educate their children privately, but enforcing boarding-school education may depend on whether or not the husband or wife were sent away to school. But the courts would not impose school fees on a man who is not earning enough income to cater for his own needs and those of his former wife and children, whatever his former wife wants.

COURT WELFARE OFFICERS

When the court is not happy with the arrangements made for the children it may order its own welfare officer to file a report, to help decide which parent will have residence, or in cases where contact arrangements are being disputed.

Sometimes a parent will ask for a report as a means of sorting out the arrangements, believing that he or she will get a sympathetic hearing. Think twice before you do this. Do you want your children to go to a court to answer a lot of intimate questions asked by a person whom they have never previously met? Sometimes welfare officers will be prepared to go to the children's home, but at other times they expect the children to see them at court.

These encounters can come as a shock to a family which has always thought itself self-sufficient. 'How can outsiders know what is best for us and our children? They haven't a clue about how we live or what our friends are like and what our interests are.'

But welfare officers are trained to look at the set-up from the children's point of view – not the parents' – irrespective of the social class of the family. A husband, for example, may say that his wife's sexual behaviour leaves too much to be desired for the stability and security of the children; she is constantly bringing strange men back to the house. Other husbands simply do not believe their former wives can cope with managing the children. Husbands also tend to fight if the wife goes to live with someone they do not like.

A wife may argue that her husband's drinking endangers the children. Parental conduct may not have been at issue when the divorce was petitioned, because there were sufficient grounds without it. A husband may be surprised to find himself labelled an alcoholic and to find his wife claiming that she fears for the children being with him and without her.

Now she could be quite right, but the welfare officer has to decide whether her objections don't in truth stem from the fact that she does not want to lose control. Is the husband really incapable of looking after his children, even for 24 hours? Is he really that dangerous?

LOSS OF AND CHANGES IN RESIDENCE ARRANGEMENTS

Once it has been decided which parent the children are to live with it is unlikely that a court would sanction a change in the arrangement because of the disruption this would cause the children. However, there is nothing to prevent parents agreeing to a change in the arrangements, always assuming that this is in accordance with the children's best interests. If, for example, a mother wants her former husband to have the children, after she has looked after them for a few years, and he has remarried and his new wife is happy, that will be acceptable. Also, on occasions when a mother becomes ill, the switch will take place.

A woman must be careful not to be seen to be abandoning her children if she wants to have them to live with her. A wife who leaves her children and her husband because she can no longer bear living with him, and sees her departure as the only solution, will have an uphill battle getting a residence order – even if there were nowhere for her to take the children.

In a case such as this, once the woman has left the family home there could be a longish delay before a court hearing. By the time it eventually takes place her husband will have had a chance to sort himself out, to have made arrangements for someone to look after the children or to have shown that he can do it himself. His wife has then to prove that she can make better arrangements for the children, or persuade the court that her husband should leave the home so that she can move back.

Unless her husband leaves voluntarily, the wife will have great difficulties. She will have to explain why she left her children, her husband will have to be made to move out of the house, and she will have to prove that this further disruption will not harm the children. So, a mother should always aim to take her children with her if she really must go, unless, for example, her husband is violent only towards her and she believes that although she must leave to protect her own safety he does not pose any risk to their children.

Mothers can also be denied contact when the children are living with their father and he can demonstrate that she is not up to looking after them – even for short periods. A mother might have had a nervous breakdown or been in and out of psychiatric hospital. In these circumstances the mother does not lose contact with her children forever. If her health improves and she can show that her breakdown was a result of the marriage, rather than from looking after the children, she will, at the very least, have reasonable contact granted.

But the court would already have decided what was best for the children irrespective of what effect the husband's personality had on either her or the children. And it would not be enough for the mother to prove that she was capable of looking after her children again – a change involving moving in with her would inevitably disrupt their lives, and the court would be likely to believe that the status quo should be maintained. However, the mother would have much more liberal contact and the children would stay with her for long periods in the holidays.

As a final word, many parents find it difficult to accept that once they are involved in a divorce the courts have the final say on what will happen to their children. This inevitably changes the relationship that the parents have with each other. So while you are coming to some agreement with your spouse, do remember that as well as convincing each other you will have to convince a court that the arrangements you choose for your children are for the best.

10

$\mathscr{F}$INANCIAL ARRANGEMENTS FOR CHILDREN

We have already mentioned how important it is for couples to agree how they are going to look after their children – both in terms of where they live and how much time each will spend with their children (Chapter 9). We have also pointed out that when couples fall out and cannot agree, the court will intervene and may impose arrangements that neither side wants.

These same principles apply to the financial arrangements made for children: where there is any disagreement the court will decide what it considers is best for the children, and their interests will be put above yours and your spouse's.

Both you and your spouse will have to accept that your standard of living will drop after the divorce. Most of the family's income is likely to stay in the same bank but it will have to support two households: most probably the husband's on the one hand and the wife's and children's on the other, so items that you may have once thought of as essential may suddenly become luxuries and you will have to forfeit them or find other means of paying for them: holidays might become a distant memory and buying your children new bicycles impossible.

The most important considerations are where your children will live and how they will be fed, clothed and educated, so in this chapter we shall consider how their needs can still be met after the family's income is effectively reduced.

- Splitting up the family home
- Maintenance for children
- Calculating children's needs
- When the children's needs change
- Education
- Squabbles over money
- Bitterness for fathers and mothers

74

While the financial arrangements for children are strictly a separate issue to the arrangements made for the mother (who most frequently is the parent who will look after them on a day-to-day basis) they are linked. We advise you to read Chapter 8 if you have not done so already, as it will give you a clear idea of what a wife may expect for herself, in addition to what she will be given in order to care for her children.

SPLITTING UP THE FAMILY HOME

When there are children, splitting up the family home – particularly when it is the family's major asset – can be traumatic and lead to protracted arguments. There may be a substantial mortgage, and to split what capital is available in half to provide two dwellings, one large enough for the children to live in, the other big enough for the children to stay overnight, can cause a great deal of anguish. There is often not enough money to go round.

When the joint assets, including the main property, are worth below £200,000, the negotiations are almost bound to be difficult, especially when the family is based in the southeast of England, where property prices are highest. For a start, there may not be enough money to exchange a four- or five-bedroom house for a three-bedroom house and a two-bedroom flat.

When the joint assets are £400,000 or more there will be sufficient money, particularly in the current market, to buy two reasonable three- or four-bedroom houses. (These figures can be scaled down proportionately for people who live in parts of the country where property is not so expensive, but the same principles apply.)

The situation which is financially most fraught is when a wife is at home, say, with two or three small children under school age. Even if she were in a position to work she would find her income whittled away paying for child care. Separation and divorce inevitably entails a significant drop in the standard of living for the whole family, because the hard-pressed husband will continue to have to maintain his family and pay for himself to live elsewhere.

Neil and Victoria and their three children (all under six) were living in a house valued at £130,000 with a £50,000 mortgage, supported by Neil's income of £35,000. They both wanted to divorce but recognized that they were going to be considerably worse off if they did so, and therefore decided to delay proceedings until Victoria was in a position to work. Luckily Neil was able to go and live with his brother in the meantime.

Another couple, Alice and Stephen, had one child, aged 2, and lived in a small two-bedroom flat. Alice kept the flat, and with the help of her parents she was able to find a small amount of capital to give to Stephen, but he still ended up living in rented accommodation.

Fortunately, there is usually some chance of trading down, but there can be great difficulties when the wife and children cannot realistically be housed elsewhere. Quite often it will be impossible for the mother and children to find a cheaper house, bearing in mind that moving expenses, legal costs and additional fixtures and fittings may soak up 10 per cent of the value of the property being sold.

You must take into account the following expenses before you decide to sell the family home and buy other property(ies):

solicitors' costs of sale and purchase
stamp duty
bridging finance, if this is relevant
estate agents' commissions
removal costs
costs of new carpets, curtains, etc. in the new house(s)

Remember you may have to pay some of these twice or three times, if you are selling one property and buying two more.

As a rule of thumb, the lower the value of the family home the higher the chances that the wife will receive more than half the value of the house, because the wife and children will still need a house, while, it is argued, the father can live in a small flat.

Sometimes it is difficult to convince a father that this is an equitable decision, because he hopes to have the children to stay sometimes, and he will want to give them a home similar to the one they have with their mother. Fathers may also be fearful that contact may become a problem if they and their children have to be squashed into a small flat. And, as Kevin – a 41-year-old divorced man whose former wife looked after their two young children – succinctly said: 'Why should I work hard all day to support my wife and children if all I get at the end of the day is a one-bedroom flat?'

Nevertheless, the courts are unyielding. In cases where the family house has a low value, wives and children may expect to receive between two-thirds and three-quarters of the capital. Judges will do their utmost to make sure that the mother and the children are adequately housed.

The general aim is to make sure that the children have secure accommodation until they are 18. In the past a judge might have made an order allowing Kevin's wife, Beth, to stay in the house with the children until the youngest child reached the age of 18, delaying the sale and division of the proceeds until then. Unless Beth remarried or there was some other dramatic change in her financial situation, the house could not be sold until that time.

These orders have gone out of fashion in the last few years, because by waiting until the children are 18 the wife then may face real difficulties rehousing herself, due to the rapid rise in house prices, and the husband very often needs some of the capital to enable himself to be rehoused. This could simply postpone the problem. So now the courts try to give both the wife and the father some share of the equity by the time the divorce is finalized.

More commonly, a wife may have a limited clean break. If, for example, the youngest child is 10, the husband might have to pay maintenance to his wife for 8 years. During that time his wife may go back to court to have the maintenance varied, but the husband knows that at the end of that time there will be a clean break. This sort of arrangement is common when there is not enough money to give the wife an immediate clean break.

Once the house is sold, and the equity divided, the husband may still end up – by adequately housing his former wife and children – paying the mortgage for his wife. This will come out of her maintenance.

MAINTENANCE FOR CHILDREN
Calculating the maintenance for children is, frankly, a bit of a lottery. The circumstances for two families may look the same, but in reality they are different and different maintenance payments may be made. Moreover, if the same family appeared before two judges they might find rather different decisions being made on the two occasions.

For some families, the position will change as a consequence of the Child Support Act 1991. Although the Act will not be implemented until 1993, it may affect some arrangements that are being made now. The discussion that follows is based on the current law. The implications of the 1991 Act are discussed in detail at the end of this chapter.

There used to be a principle that a wife could expect a third of the joint income before tax, with the children receiving a third and the husband the last third. In practice, unless school fees are taken into account, children would rarely receive as much as a third. While this fractional approach has fallen out of favour, solicitors still need to have some starting point on which to base their negotiations.

Now the approach is to assess what are the reasonable needs and requirements of the wife and children; and then the reasonable needs and requirements of the husband. Although the wife's and the children's maintenance are rolled into a single monthly payment, there has to be some notion of what the split is between the wife and children – just in case the wife remarries and the husband then only has to pay for the children.

In the days before the 1987 budget, when maintenance payments were tax deductible, a child's tax-free income allowance was the benchmark, which a few years ago was £2,400 per annum. That commonly was the level of maintenance for a child for a great number of families – irrespective of their circumstances, whether the husband earned £20,000 or £200,000. While that figure has risen with inflation some solicitors still think in the region of £2,500 to £3,000 per child per year.

Many more solicitors recognize that applying this sort of formula is rather short-sighted: the cost of keeping a 3-year-old is rather less than the cost of keeping a 16-year-old. So while the lowest maintenance agreed for the children of fathers earning from £20,000 to £200,000 is still about £2,000, the highest, excluding arrangements made by the richest families, would be about £5,000 per child.

Some mothers demand £5,000 or £6,000 for a 4-year-old, but they are highly unlikely to receive that amount, particularly if there are, say, three children in the family and the father is paying school fees separately. Most solicitors would accept that a mother who receives £5,000 on behalf of each of her children is doing very well indeed. Remember that children who command £5,000 may well be at a boarding school, so it is likely that their mother will only have to look after them for just over four months every year in the holidays, and the children are likely to spend some of that time with their father.

One solicitor commented that the highest maintenance award he had come across where the circumstances were not particularly unusual was £6,000 per child. In another case the husband agreed to pay £1,000 per child per month, but he expected his children to visit him abroad and travel with him.

Solicitors acting for mothers may start the negotiation at around £3,500 to £4,000 for each child. To get more, mothers would have to do a detailed schedule showing that the children indulge in, say, an expensive sport, or have costly holidays. Even fathers with huge incomes may not have a great deal of spare income because their own lifestyle is likely to be expensive and they will be reluctant to forfeit much of it.

Husbands often do not like paying too much maintenance, as they resent their wives spending money on the children when they want to be able to spend the money themselves. They may also feel that they are subsidizing the second husband of their former wife, if she receives a large cheque every month on behalf of their children.

Some husbands do not want to pay set amounts each month at all – they do not like being ordered to pay, and want to be seen to be giving out of the generosity of their own hearts. They want to be presented with bills so they can see exactly where the money is going. This can be achieved, provided both husband and wife are happy with the arrangement, and provided the husband will always pay the bills without argument.

Solicitors and judges do not encourage these arrangements, believing that wives will be more secure if they have a regular income on behalf of their children. If, on top of a small maintenance payment, husbands and wives are happy to discuss larger bills less frequently, that may work. But, however good relations are, if you have to discuss bills every few months, there is bound to be some friction.

CALCULATING CHILDREN'S NEEDS

In the same way that wives are asked to draw up a list of their own needs (see Chapter 6), mothers should consider their children's financial needs. For children you look at pocket money, extra-curricular school activities (one-off outings), children's activities (such as swimming or visits to the zoo), holidays, the cost of clothes, special events like birthday parties and Christmas treats and entertainment – in short anything that the children have come to expect. Do not forget to include costs which will be 'new' in the sense that your former spouse, say, used to drive the children to school and now, because you cannot drive, they will have to go by bus.

This list will then be sent to the husband and the arguments will begin over whether or not the children really have so much spent on them.

Maintenance for children usually includes
- Day-to-day food and expenses
- Clothes – not school uniforms
- Pocket money
- Family outings – including travel costs
- Holidays with their mother

Maintenance usually excludes
- School fees, uniforms and extras; special tuition during the holidays

A father will usually have financial responsibility for maintenance and school fees, even when his wife has a good salary. The courts have the power to make an order that will run until the children finish full-time education.

WHEN THE CHILDREN'S NEEDS CHANGE

Discussions start all over again when there is a change of circumstances for the children. When their mother remarries, for example, the children's needs will be reassessed. This will happen even when the mother has received a clean break capital sum, because the children's needs will alter if they are rehoused with their mother and her new husband.

Most importantly, it must be remembered that the court does not have any powers to dismiss the children's claims; it can only dismiss a wife's claim for herself. Children, or their mothers on their behalf, can return to court as often as they wish.

Some wealthy families opt to establish a trust fund to pay for their children's maintenance and education, the capital then becoming available to them, say, when they are 25. But whatever arrangements are made, the courts may still review the arrangements in the years to come. Say a husband put £500,000 in a trust for his children and it was badly invested and gradually became devalued: they would always have the opportunity to go back via the court to ask their father for further funds.

EDUCATION

One major expense in some families is school fees, so you might be prepared to forfeit private education for your children if a divorce will involve a significant drop in the standard of living for you and your spouse. But many parents find this a particularly difficult decision to take and, interestingly, husbands and wives who may disagree on everything else will often admit that they are both committed to private education and will bend over backwards to make sure that their children continue at the same schools.

Once the children are 18, and provided they are still in full-time education, some maintenance will need to be sorted out, and children can make their own applications.

University grants are based on the income of the parent with whom the child lives – usually the mother. In the past this has been a windfall for divorced couples, because when the wife has a limited income the grant will be paid in full. Parents and children should also know that any maintenance will be deducted from the grant, so fathers should not pay under an order but make voluntary gifts to their children instead.

Sometimes children cannot benefit from a grant and, sadly, it is not unusual for fathers to say that they are no longer prepared to pay for older children, in which case the children will have to take their fathers to court, with obvious unhappy repercussions.

SQUABBLES OVER MONEY

The problem is, of course, that when a mother draws up her list of the things she considers her children need, the total sum may come to more money than the couple have! This is why some fathers start querying the cost of haircuts or of school tights. Other common bones of contention for people to watch for are child care bills, costs of parties and weekend outings, and what holidays the mother should take with the children.

Geoffrey used to despair when his children came to stay for the weekend: 'I give my former wife lots of money yet my children turn up appallingly dressed.' He had to be reminded that something drove him and his wife Juliet apart – namely that they wanted rather different lifestyles. Geoffrey was more concerned by appearances, and wanted his children to be turned out well. His second wife, Sian, was more sophisticated and clothes-conscious than Juliet, and often took the children out on a shopping spree. Juliet, on the other hand, preferred to spend money on cultural events and could not care less about clothes. Differences are not going to go away just because a couple is divorced.

BITTERNESS FOR FATHERS AND MOTHERS

With increasing opportunities for women to follow demanding and well-paid careers, husbands might reasonably expect to receive an equal share of the family's assets, particularly if both parents have played a large part in bringing up the children. This is not yet reflected in divorce settlements.

The prevalent view is that a man should be slow to claim against his wife, although that may change with time. Even when a wife is much richer than her husband his claim would never be as great as his wife's if the financial tables were reversed. Significant awards are not made in favour of men, whatever the means of the wife. Men will still be provided with accommodation, but the award will be less generous than a wife might expect if the financial tables were turned. The wife is likely to have the children living with her, and that will be a hefty factor in apportioning money.

So, irrespective of what a wife earns or her private means, the working husband still is looked upon as the major supporter for the children. Gillian and Adam were both senior executives, earning over £60,000 each. It is quite likely that the court would believe that Adam could pay maintenance and school fees without impoverishing himself. Gillian would also be expected to make a sizeable contribution to the care of the children.

Their financial equality would be taken into account in apportioning capital. While the legal statutes do not distinguish between men and women (they are both called spouses), and in theory a husband's rights are equal those of his wife, in practice they are not. A husband will not get the same amount of capital as a wife would if their positions were reversed.

THE EFFECT OF THE CHILD SUPPORT ACT 1991

This Act is unlikely to take effect until 1993, but it may be important to be aware now of its impact.

The Act creates an entirely new framework for the assessment and collection of maintenance for children. Its purpose is to eliminate the current uncertainty about how much should be paid to children, and to improve collection of payments.

The main features of the Act are as follows:

- all parents, married or not, are liable under the Act to support their natural children (but not step-children);
- child support will be assessed and enforced by a government Child Support Agency;
- the levels of child support will be fixed by a statutory calculation;
- the court will be prevented, except in certain cases, from making orders for child maintenance.

Since the level of child support that will be required is comparatively low (because it is based on Income Support and related Benefit rates), the main impact of the Act will be on poorer families. However, the following points need to be borne in mind.

The prohibition on courts making orders for child support means that the statutory formula will have to be the starting point in *every* case. When the parties are in the middle – or upper – income or asset bracket, the court *may* make orders additional to the statutory formula. They may also confirm agreed orders, provided that the child support element is at least that required by the Act; and they may make orders to cover the costs of a child's education or the extra cost incurred in caring for a disabled child.

The immediate implication of this is that everyone should now ensure that what is agreed to be paid to the children should be at *least* the equivalent of that which would be ordered after 1993 by the Agency. Failure to do this may mean that the liable parent (usually the father) who has, say, agreed to forego his share in the house in return for making no support to his children, or reduced payments, may find that he will later be forced by the Agency to pay the statutory rate. This could come as an unpleasant shock.

11

$\mathscr{R}$ETIREMENT AND DEATH

Pensions, life assurance and wills

A generation or two ago, few people would expect to live to their eighties. In the 1990s that is quite common, and so those who are divorcing after a long marriage must take a hard look at how they are both going to survive – financially – in their old age.

There are now thousands of marriages that collapse just after the couple's children have left home, when husband and wife are in their fifties. Care must be taken to make sure that both parties will have enough money to live separately, possibly for as long as 30 years. In addition, there are increasing numbers of people in their sixties and seventies who, even after 30 or 40 years of marriage, realize that they may have 10 or 15 years of life left and want to start afresh, either on their own or with someone else. These people are unlikely to be working and earning a salary, so pension arrangements are critical for couples who divorce in their fifties or older.

PENSIONS

For pension arrangements to be considered as part of the financial settlement the pension is usually anticipated in the foreseeable future, i.e. it is unlikely to be more than 10 years or so away. When both husband and wife are in their early forties it is extremely difficult to value the husband's pension: he might change jobs; he might lose his job – anything can happen – and women below the age of 45 are, in general, considered to have a fair chance of building up their own pensions.

Not surprisingly, pensions play no part in short marriages, when the couple is young and have no children.

The older you are, therefore, the more your or your spouse's pension dominates the financial arrangements. At the moment, wives are particularly vulnerable because, in the vast majority of divorces, the woman either has no pension, or, if she has her own, it is likely to be much smaller than her husband's. Moreover, she is statistically likely to outlive her former husband by some years. In the future, as more couples divorce where both parties have had careers and pensions, this picture will change.

The current problems lie in the divorce courts' inability to change the often strict rules laid down by pension schemes which state who can benefit. The trustees of the pension scheme cannot take decisions outside these rules, although some schemes are more flexible than others; the courts have no power over the trustees, and they cannot order a husband to specify that his former wife should receive a pension. The most the courts can do is to order him to compensate his former wife for her future loss from other capital which he may have.

Many schemes state that on the death of a member after retirement the widow will be entitled to a proportion of the pension – usually about half. When there is no wife the pension may be paid to his surviving children (if they are under the age of 18) or to any dependent adult, for example if the couple had a mentally handicapped child. Some schemes do allow a former wife to be classified as a 'dependent adult' if she is receiving maintenance, and this is often the best safety net available. If the scheme does not allow this, the rules leave the man's former wife out in the cold; her prospects are even gloomier if her husband has remarried. Once decree absolute is granted a former wife cannot become a widow when her former husband dies and she loses all benefits; this is one of the very unfair things about divorce as things presently stand.

One Civil Service pension scheme is particularly iniquitous, as Bill found to his cost. He wanted to divorce and remarry a woman in her early forties, but decided against it when he looked into his pension and found that if he did everyone was going to lose out.

He discovered that when he died his second wife, Elizabeth, would receive only a third of what Alison, his first wife, might have expected had they remained married. Alison, on the other hand, would receive nothing from the pension fund. Bill decided not to divorce, even though he desperately wanted to, and instead he and Alison had a judicial separation. He now lives with Elizabeth, and although he is unable to marry her he has made special arrangements in his will to ensure that she will benefit from his estate when he dies. Alison for her part will continue to have the security of the widow's pension.

Some pension schemes would not even allow this arrangement. The former wife might receive no benefits because they are only payable to the widow when she and her husband are 'married and living together at the date of retirement'. In these cases, the couple may be advised to postpone either the whole divorce or the decree absolute until after the husband retires.

There are, mercifully, a number of ways a divorcing woman in her fifties or sixties (and her solicitor) can try to ensure that she will have sufficient money for her old age.

Flexible pension schemes

First, get hold of a copy of the rules covering your or your spouse's pension scheme and a recent statement, showing the current value of the pension and its estimated value at the time of retirement: both the value of the annual pension and the value of the tax-free lump sum which is likely to be payable.

You may find that the pension is flexible and that your husband (if it is his pension) can nominate you as a beneficiary on his death. Some schemes, for example, allow a man to give up part of his own pension to provide a pension to his former spouse after his death. If it is not flexible, the figures will at least give you some grounds for negotiation.

Clean breaks

As we have seen, pension arrangements start to be crucial when a wife is in her late forties or early fifties and her husband is the same age or older. She can see her husband's pension in sight and the pension fund may look huge, but it is difficult to give a realistic value for a pension which will not become payable for another 10 years or more. The potential income from a pension which the wife will lose on divorce may be the deciding factor that brings about a clean break.

Where the money is available, a wife will be looking for a handsome sum to make up for her loss of pension rights and, where possible, a clean break is without doubt the best option. The main advantage is that a wife does not have to worry about her husband making adequate provision for her out of his estate to prevent her being left high and dry when he dies.

Although there are no strict rules at present for calculating what lump sum a wife needs to make up for her loss of pension rights, by forfeiting her rights to the pension a wife in her late fifties can be entitled to as much as 70 to 80 per cent of the family's capital assets, according to the latest figures. Much really depends on how much money is around which can be paid to the wife.

The disadvantage to a husband of a clean break after a long marriage is that it is expensive: it is possible that all assets have to be reduced to cash, however rich the couple may seem.

For example, Jack, an oil company executive who had a £65,000 index-linked pension and apparent assets of £1.5 million (including the matrimonial home), could not afford a clean break! There was not enough money to provide two reasonable houses and give his wife a lump sum sufficient to provide her with adequate income for the future. In order to provide the sum that would have been acceptable he would have had to sell assets in addition to the home, and that would have attracted punitive capital gains tax.

Capital gains tax can be a problem for a divorcing couple if the settlement involves the transfer of property (other than the matrimonial home) or shares from one party to the other. If matters are not sorted out during the financial year in which the parties have separated, the capital gains tax exemptions that normally exist between husband and wife disappear.

What older wives should do with their lump sum

Sensible wives may well purchase an annuity with either part or all of their lump sum. This will give them an income for life – whether they live for a further five years or 25 years – and the certainty and security that they will not have to worry about money. The disadvantage of an annuity is that it is inflexible and if the wife dies after only a couple of years the money which the couple's children could have inherited will have been wasted buying the annuity – which is inevitably expensive. The alternative is to find a good broker who will invest the lump sum and try to achieve a proper balance between income now and capital growth for the future to protect against inflation.

When a lump sum cannot be paid immediately

The vast majority of men do not have enough capital (other than the matrimonial home) to give their former wives a lump sum instantly. In these cases there are a number of options open to them.

Borrowing

Some husbands raise bank loans in order to finance a clean break now, anticipating that when they retire, their own pension lump sum will more than cover the loan and interest.

Increase the wife's share in the matrimonial home

A husband might agree to increase his wife's share in the matrimonial home so that she could sell it after the divorce, buy somewhere smaller and invest the balance. Even this may not give her enough for a completely clean break, however.

For example, Frances was given the matrimonial home, which was worth £150,000. She and Patrick agreed that she would only sell it when her children left university (two years after the divorce). Although she kept the cash to compensate her for the loss of pension benefits, her solicitor was concerned that after buying a small flat for £90,000 she would not have enough to invest and live on for 20 or 30 years. Frances and Patrick were a classic example of a couple who could not really afford to divorce because Patrick could not afford to give her any more capital.

Deferred payment

In certain circumstances the wife's application for a lump sum can be deferred until the pension comes through, although this is unlikely if that will not happen for more than four or five years. To defer for a longer period would mean neither side knowing where he or she stood in the meantime.

Gregory and Hattie divorce, for example, when Gregory is 61 and Hattie 57, four years before Gregory's retirement. Hattie should be able to claim part of the lump sum due to Gregory when he retires. It may be worth while for Hattie to defer her application for a lump sum until Gregory has retired, when the precise amount of the lump sum will be known.

Flexible payment

The husband could pay half the lump sum on divorce and the rest when he retires at 65. The trouble with this type of arrangement is that the woman may lose out. If her former husband has to retire early, the lump sum may not be quite as large as she expected, or if he wants to work longer his former wife may have to wait so long for her lump sum that she falls into debt.

Delaying application

In exceptional circumstances a woman might not make any application for a lump sum until some years after the divorce. In one case, for example, a wife made no application because her husband was an undischarged bankrupt. Nine years later he inherited some money when his father died and his former wife then applied for a lump sum, which was successful – because her former husband had made no maintenance payments in the intervening years.

Maintenance

As we have explained, a clean break is a good idea if the couple have a lot of money. Many women, however, feel that they will be better off with maintenance than a lump sum, provided that they have adequate security for income once their former husband dies and maintenance comes to an end.

Receiving reasonable maintenance from a former husband with an index-linked pension of about £60,000 a year (which is not that unusual) can be more appealing than a lump sum payment which is vulnerable to stock-market fluctuations and to high rates of tax.

Protection for wives on maintenance

As we have seen, under the rules of some pension schemes, a husband can nominate a former wife as a dependant so both she and his widow can be beneficiaries of any lump sum or pension payable on his death.

Life assurance

A wife can arrange for an appropriate life assurance policy to be taken out on her former husband's life. Because the person she is taking out the policy on is no longer her husband, however, she can only insure the amount of money she would lose by his death (not an unlimited sum), and this inevitably involves some guesswork.

Charge on estate

At the time of divorce, a husband can agree to his former wife having a charge on his property, so that when he dies his estate will be certain of having the funds to pay a lump sum to her. This is unpopular if the husband remarries because it restricts what his new family will gain. An alternative is for the husband to agree to make suitable provision for his former wife in his will, but this may be unsatisfactory to her; the husband may not have enough money in his estate when he dies to meet her needs, and there is also the risk that he may change his will in the meantime.

Death in service benefit

Some pension schemes, particularly company schemes, provide for a lump sum (often four times annual salary) to be paid to a husband's family if he dies while in employment; it may be possible for the husband to nominate his former wife as a beneficiary of part of the lump sum; this will give her some protection, at least while the husband is working.

If no provision has been made, a wife can apply to the court on her former husband's death for an order under the Inheritance (Provision for Family and Dependants) Act 1975 against his estate to make sure she will not starve. There is no time limit on when she does so, provided that i) she has not remarried, ii) she can show that she was dependent on him through maintenance payments, and iii) there are sufficient assets in the estate. The court has a great deal of discretion and will look at a number of factors, including the needs of the husband's new family, when deciding what his former wife should receive.

Section 10 application

If a woman thinks that she is not going to be given a reasonable settlement, she can make a Section 10 application – although this is a last resort. This application (so-called because it comes under Section 10 of the Matrimonial Causes Act 1973) is a tactical step that can be taken by a wife who is a respondent if, for example, she is concerned that the divorce will mean that she loses out over her husband's pension and no realistic suggestions have been made by the husband to deal with her loss. The decree absolute cannot then be granted until the district judge is satisfied that her husband is going to make the best provisions that can be made in the circumstances. All Section 10 does is to preserve widow's rights until the best available solution is found; the decree absolute will still need to be granted to make the financial order effective.

Severe financial hardship

In rare cases (and only when the divorce petition is based on 5 years separation), a woman may be able to prove that she will suffer such grave financial hardship through the loss of access to her husband's pension that the divorce should not take place – not like Bill and Alison who voluntarily decided not to divorce, but in circumstances when a district judge will not grant a decree because of the likelihood of the wife's real poverty. This is a desperate measure and the couple should look closely at the other ways of protecting the wife's position, as outlined above.

INSURANCE POLICIES

Insurance policies might also be considered by younger divorcing couples, who are not so concerned about protecting pension rights.

For younger women, a short-term endowment policy is worth considering so that it matures when the woman needs an injection of money – for example, when either she or her former husband retires. There are occasional difficulties if the wife suddenly cannot afford to pay the premiums. The husband will not want to pay if he has given his wife a clean break and her rights have been dismissed, or if she has remarried. If at all possible, the wife should be given money on divorce to make sure all premiums will be paid.

A parent (usually the father) who does not look after the children on a day-to-day basis may want to take out an insurance policy on the life of his former spouse so that if she were to die while the children were still dependent some money would be available to cover the extra expense of looking after them while he continued to work. Usually this will be a 'term' policy and only last as long as the children remain dependent because the premiums will be much lower than for a 'whole life' policy.

WILLS

Divorce affects wills; any reference to a wife or husband in a will is invalid after decree absolute and so it is important to make a new will before decree absolute is granted. It is sensible, in any event, to make a new will once divorce proceedings are under way, because if your existing will leaves your estate to your husband or wife (as is usual), it is unlikely that you are going to continue to want him or her to benefit once divorce is on the cards. If you have never made a will it is important to do so since otherwise, if you were to die before decree absolute is granted, a proportion of your estate would pass automatically to your husband or wife, under the intestacy rules.

STATE PENSIONS

The payment of the basic state pension to a divorced woman depends on her age when she divorces and on whether it is based on her own or her former husband's contributions – or a combination of both.

For example, Sheila was 59 when she and Iain started divorce proceedings. She was advised to time the decree absolute until a few days after her 60th birthday so that she could qualify for a full pension without making any contributions herself. Full details about pensions for women who are widowed or divorced are available on pages 50 and 58 in DSS Guide leaflet NP46.

12
*O*THER FINANCIAL ARRANGEMENTS

Chattels, trusts and family companies

The assets for many people going through a divorce are clearly defined and easily realizable, however painful the process. There is the family house (possibly two, if the family is comfortably off), a car (or two), a boat perhaps, some shares, and possibly some paintings and antique furniture. If necessary, everything can be converted into cash and the proceeds divided.

Sorting out a couple's financial affairs becomes complicated when the assets are either in trust, their lifestyle is subsidized by other members of the family, or the husband's company or their assets are tied up in a family business or in land, the value of which is uncertain.

HEIRLOOMS, COLLECTED ITEMS AND CHATTELS

Pictures and furniture in houses, however valuable, are not usually considered saleable assets and part of the bargaining in a divorce settlement. The contents of the family home will rarely be sold to raise cash unless there are some items that are extremely valuable and the couple cannot agree as to who will take them. Commonly, chattels are divided by agreement – not because of their cash value.

Selling of objets d'art only becomes an issue when there are not enough other assets which can be realized to support two smaller households. For example, Mark owned some eighteenth-century porcelain which had been in his family for five generations. His solicitors had to decide, because the porcelain was not a cash asset, which was more important – keeping the porcelain or meeting his wife's needs. His wife came first.

Only if the heirlooms were a national treasure would the wife's needs come second. Some furniture which was an integral part of a house to which the public had access might perhaps be preserved.

Donald had a collection of vintage cars which he had built up during his marriage. When he and his wife Claire divorced there was no reason (other than Donald's own love for them) that the cars should not be sold.

Donald had to struggle to keep them because he had to find the cash equivalent to share with Claire.

None of this stops couples arguing over particular possessions, which often turn out to have been wedding presents. The divorce proceedings have gone through smoothly, the couple have agreed amicably on how they will look after their children and what will happen to their house. The battle starts when either the husband or wife is looking for an opportunity of having a go at the other and all other chances of retribution are slipping away.

In extreme cases the ground rules for the argument seem quite petty, particularly when the item in question was bought during the marriage. A woman may claim that she found the dining-room table, but the husband wants it because he paid for it. Just occasionally, the solicitors for both sides will have to send an articled clerk to the matrimonial home to keep the couple apart while each item is discussed.

An art dealer and his wife had a reasonably amicable divorce except for a dispute over nine paintings. She wanted them to adorn her new house, he refused because he had collected them. The couple had to be persuaded that it was not worth going to court over them.

Relations between husband and wife can hardly be lower than when they fight over possessions. It is not unknown for husbands and wives to raid each other's homes and claim disputed possessions. Neither is it uncommon for there to be court proceedings over chattels and for one side to threaten to take items or dispose of them. There are even occasions where an injunction has been made to stop one side selling some object.

When a couple has to go to court over the chattels, something has gone seriously wrong, as it is likely that the legal costs of either party or in aggregate will be greater than the value of the chattels being fought over. The chances are that both sides were badly advised and, however frustrating the arguments, the parties are more likely to be satisfied by an out-of-court agreement. A decision imposed by a judge is likely to backfire on both sides.

In less-heated circumstances, and if the wife and the couple's children are staying in the matrimonial home, she will acquire most of the functional items, such as the kitchen appliances, beds, etc. It is more sensible for a wife to have them because she has to be able to look after the children and it would be expensive if she had to go and buy them anew. It is also considered easier for husbands, who are probably living in a smaller place, to gradually build things up again.

So, in practice, a woman might be given the entire contents of the house, minus a few pictures, bits of furniture and her husband's books and record collection. However, if they have a painting worth £10,000 or so, there is a case for it being sold and the cash divided.

TRUSTS AND CASH BENEFITS

Trusts are only relevant in a divorce when the income makes a difference to the couple's standard of living – or will do in the future. The trouble is that the beneficiary of a trust cannot change the terms of the trust – that is the responsibility of the trustees. This is further complicated because a judge in a divorce court has no jurisdiction over the trustees of a discretionary trust and cannot order the trustees to make a distribution (payment from the trust) to a potential beneficiary.

The only way a judge can force trustees to make a distribution is to make life so financially difficult for the beneficiary that the trustees will then decide that they have to meet his or her new demands. If you benefit from a trust it is absolutely essential that you have tip-top legal advice, which can ensure you and your spouse will be treated fairly.

Andrew was among a number of people who were discretionary beneficiaries of a large trust, and received huge distributions throughout his marriage. His wife's solicitors were informed that the trustees were going to make no further distributions if she was going to benefit from them. The judge accepted their right to refuse to make further payments to Andrew but ordered that his extremely valuable stamp collection and library, which were not owned by the trust, should be sold to provide a fund to produce a source of income for his wife to claim against.

People may have a life interest in a trust, in which case they will receive the income from the trust throughout their lifetimes, whatever their personal or other circumstances. If, however, they are discretionary beneficiaries, the trustees may or may not give them a regular income. The courts will want to know in which way they have benefited, and they can order the disclosure of the terms of the trust.

James and Diana had been married for 15 years. Although James had a good salary, the family had been well supplemented by the income from Diana's family trust. When they decided to divorce, James argued successfully that he should receive a lump sum settlement from Diana of

£150,000, a sum which she in turn claimed she could not afford and did not have access to because it was tied up in the trust.

The judge decided that Diana could afford that sum easily, believing the trust was a sham, although she would have to bring pressure on the trustees to change the terms so that she could continue to live comfortably herself.

Simon and Helena were divorcing after 20 years of marriage. Simon and his solicitor argued that Helena did not require a large lump sum settlement because Helena's mother was the beneficiary of a trust which had been in her family for years. In due course, Helena would become the sole beneficiary of the trust on her mother's death. The court accepted Simon's argument and Helena had to accept a relatively small lump sum.

Divorces when couples are still relatively young – in their forties – and who have been subsidized by one set of parents through regular cash hand outs, can cause a great deal of distress. Had the marriage survived the couple might have expected to inherit the wealth, but not necessarily.

If the parents are likely to die in the foreseeable future (if they are frail and elderly), their wealth will have some bearing on the divorce settlement. For example, Louis, his former wife and their solicitors agreed that while at the point of divorce he did not have enough money to make her a realistic lump sum settlement, he would give her a fifth of whatever he received when his parents died.

However, if the parents are fit and energetic and likely to live for 20 years or so, their former son- or daughter-in-law cannot expect to benefit from their wealth for a number of reasons.

For a start, their fortune could decline. The money may be badly invested; the parents may suffer from a terrible illness which whittles away their assets; or perhaps the wealthy parents' child could fall out of favour and be cut out of the will.

When wealth is a simple question of inheritance there is no certainty that the children will receive any of the fortune. Only when there is a vested interest in a trust which will definitely pass down the generations can a divorcing couple take this income into account.

Perks

Men and women who are apparently wealthy may not have large salaries: they may just happen to work in a sector where there are massive perks. Perks must always be taken into consideration during a divorce. A company car, which most businessmen and -women expect, is of great benefit and their former spouse may have benefited from it as well. A person may also have a massive expense account.

The less well-off party to a divorce should examine his or her partner's bank statements when that partner has a lifestyle not supported by income alone, to try to find out how it has been maintained. A monthly salary may not be a true indication of the partner's worth – in the most extreme cases the salary may be effectively 'pocket money', all other living expenses being met by the company.

FAMILY COMPANIES AND ESTATES

When a husband's or wife's assets are tied up in a family company or in, say, a large working family farm, rather different deals have to be struck. On paper the family may seem extremely wealthy, but the wealth cannot be liquidated because it would mean the business would have to be broken up or the farm sold and too many other people's livelihoods – in the extended family – would be jeopardized.

For a start, selling a family estate or company would attract enormous tax liabilities – capital gains tax and/or corporation tax. The sale of a house which had been in the same family for 250 years, for example, might raise cash, but there would be great losses to the couple's children which could never be recouped.

So there is little point in appointing expensive accountants to investigate the value of a landed estate or a company when it is quite clear that it will not be sold. And it is meaningless to discuss what a family is worth if their extended family depends on the income from the company estate.

A couple who have lived on a farm on an estate have had obvious financial advantages while they were married, because their housing costs were subsidized. They are at a considerable financial disadvantage when their marriage fails because it is impossible to realize that asset (the house) and difficult to get a sufficient income out of the farm to support two families. The problems are accentuated when the couple has little income but receives lots of benefits, and where most of the running costs of the house are met by the farm company.

In these circumstances solicitors have to look at the problem from a different angle, and consider the couple's needs and those of their children. There is little point in considering what the family is worth on paper; instead the solicitors must look at practical ways in which the two families can live separately.

For example, a couple may have lived in a large house that has been in one family for many hundreds of years. That will, obviously, stay in the family (and it makes no difference if it is the husband's or wife's family). Solicitors investigate whether or not a small part of the land could be sold off to house either the husband or the wife and children. Cottages and barns can be converted or sold to raise money to pay for a new house.

Alternatively, solicitors will find out whether money can be raised on the security of the estate. Can this land be sold without ruining the whole farm? Can a husband raise a mortgage on the farm in order to house his wife and children elsewhere? Clearly the person having to leave the original house is unlikely to live as graciously as he or she did before, but at least will always have a roof over his or her head.

In these circumstances (when all the family's assets are tied up) the wife is unlikely to be given a clean break – the estate could keep her going on a month-to-month basis but could not find a huge lump sum to set her up independently in a way that would make her happy. Even if she were offered £500,000, her solicitor would be likely to advise her to ask for a house and maintenance instead.

If a wife is offered a different property on the estate but does not want to live so close to the old matrimonial home she can demand that the property be sold, so that she can live much further away – although she might lose some benefits of staying on the estate, such as help in the garden or access to odd-job help.

The preservation of the estate is not always the number-one priority – the needs of the children and wife must be met first. But solicitors will always take into account the children's future, which may be better served if the estate is left intact, so that they will be able to enjoy it when they are older.

Some land-owning families are already so deeply in debt – the estate is already overdrawn and the family has been living off capital for years – that the divorce may trigger the break-up of the estate. In these circumstances, the divorce is an additional financial burden which simply cannot be met. Similarly, some family companies may be on the brink of collapse and a divorce tips the balance. There is no option but to sell the remaining parts of the business.

When the company or estate has benefited from the marriage, a husband who has built up his wife's assets or who has managed the family estate well for the wife can expect a more generous settlement than a husband who has run his wife's estate badly and has landed a family company with a large liability.

LIQUID ASSETS ABROAD

In multinational divorces it is not unusual for financial proceedings to take place in another country. Courts have, in theory, the power to make decisions affecting a couple's worldwide assets. One obvious problem, however, is tracing these foreign assets or enforcing any order in respect of them. Can we be sure that the husband has disclosed all his assets, particularly if he has been paid abroad?

Wealthy men frequently keep money in Switzerland, so it is important in cases like this to see the husband's bank statements to try to spot any transfers of assets. Even when the assets have been identified, and an order is made for the assets to be returned to the UK, the foreign country in question may not recognize the order.

It is difficult, for example, to enforce an order in, say, an Arab country or in part of the world with no European links. There is a reasonable chance of freezing assets held in the United States, although you have to take account of US Federal Law when you are acting for a wife. Solicitors who do not think the husband is being completely honest, and have evidence of this, usually obtain a freezing order to prevent the husband moving his assets around the world.

13
$\mathcal{M}$ISAPPREHENSIONS

Gerald was convinced that his two children, aged 11 and 9, would live with him after he and his accountant wife Janet divorced. After they had first separated he had been fortunate to find a room in a house just round the corner so that most evenings he was able to see the children, help them with their homework and put them to bed. He moved back every other weekend as well, which suited Janet, who spent this time with her new partner, Frank.

In Gerald's eyes little had changed: Janet continued to work long hours at her job, she clearly had more time for Frank than she had ever had for Gerald and the children (the fact that he had to fend for himself was not new). But Gerald was in for a shock: Janet was granted leave to take the children out of the country to live with her when her employer posted her to France, although Gerald's access arrangements were generous.

Gerald was bitterly disappointed and thought that the arrangement was deeply unfair. He had, after all, been a generous and committed husband and was very involved with his children. He found it difficult to accept that although Janet had been unfaithful and, by her own admission, a less than supportive wife, this did not mean that she was a bad mother.

Gerald's misapprehension is not unusual. As we explained in Chapters 1 and 5, increasingly there are moves to take the 'blame' out of divorce and in legal terms to consider the factors in the divorce quite separately from the arrangements made financially and for the children. However, many people either refuse to take this on board emotionally or are unable to do so.

A husband or wife who has been unceremoniously dumped for another person is bound to feel bitter and resentful. It is human nature in these circumstances to want a former spouse to suffer for his or her actions – to pay the price of his or her folly. And, as the injured party often cannot accept that the former spouse will pay any emotional price, he or she expects that spouse to pay through the children or financially.

A husband and wife who have separated in bitter circumstances will naturally look for some area where they can vent their feelings, and this can be a great source of misery if they unwittingly misapprehend the divorce proceedings.

Children, too, can be scarred forever by divorce: one parent turns them against the other and, even though access arrangements are fair, the father may be told that the children do not want to see him. Only the most brutal man will force himself on what he has been made to perceive are his reluctant children. All too frequently, a man and a woman forget that, although they are no longer husband and wife, they have a duty to continue to have some relationship with each other as parents to their children – however painful that is.

In an ideal divorce each parent will encourage contact between their children and the other parent. Frequently, however, one parent may seek to poison the children against the 'absentee' parent and to reduce their contact with him or her on the grounds that it is not in the children's interest. This is rarely justifiable save in the cases of very young children and a highly irresponsible parent. In older children, if what one parent is saying about the other is accurate it is better for the children to see and come to that decision themselves through contact with the absentee parent; if the parent's view is inaccurate the children will benefit from the contact, anyway, and the parent who is truly acting in the children's best interest should be satisfied.

MONEY

While Gerald's reaction is one of the most common misapprehensions held by men as far as residency arrangements for children are concerned, there are other misapprehensions, some of which can have devastating long-term effects.

Colin was an exemplary, if rather uninspiring, husband and father. He gave Sheena generous housekeeping and was happy for her to spend money on her appearance. But she started to have an affair, and when it came out in the open Colin thought it best to leave the family home until everything was 'back to normal'. Initially he protected Sheena and told their friends that his wife had made a mistake and they would be back together soon. He even hinted that she had gone off balance.

As the months went by, and there was no sign of reconciliation, Colin started to think that he was losing control of her. However, there was one way that he still could keep her in his power: money. He started to become very difficult over how much she should spend.

Clearly Colin's pride was hurt. He believed that if he punished Sheena by not giving her what she wanted (i.e. money) she would see the error of her ways, come to her senses and ask him back. For months he continued to believe that Sheena and he would start again.

When they inevitably came to divorce Colin was resentful of the judge's decision to award Sheena a reasonable interim maintenance award, and intended to fight to the bitter end to make sure that she received as little as possible. Any chance that there might have been of Colin and Sheena continuing to live together disappeared, something that it took a long time for Colin to accept. He did not learn that punishing and then attempting to 'rescue' Sheena would not help.

Many women, when they first go and visit a solicitor – just for advice on money and not because they really envisage a divorce – say that they do not want to start divorce proceedings but they want to frighten their husbands into coming home. Women in their forties are particularly vulnerable. They often say that their husbands are going through the male menopause (which is why they have gone off with a younger woman). While that may be true, it does not mean that if the new relationship founders their husband will come back to their wives.

It is difficult for these women to face up to the idea of a divorce petition. They need time, but after a few months, if nothing has changed, a good divorce solicitor will persuade them to start proceedings for real: their husbands are unlikely to 'come to their senses' and to stall is only delaying the inevitable.

Fear of disclosure

Misapprehensions over money often lead to real problems during divorce proceedings, and to long and ridiculous delays. A husband, say, does not want to give financial information to his wife's solicitor because he is frightened that he will lose his assets and believes that, if he keeps quiet, in the long run he will be better off. By dragging his feet he thinks he will prolong the period before which he has to hand over the lump sum or start paying hefty maintenance. This approach may backfire.

Roger was asked to settle £80,000 on his wife, Joan, but he was not prepared to do so and wanted to negotiate a different deal. Joan would not change her mind, so discussions ground to a halt. As it happened his financial circumstances improved dramatically, and by the time things were sorted out some two years later he had to give her much more.

Joyce was convinced that her husband Ben was not revealing his true financial position, and kept on instructing her solicitors to make exhaustive enquiries of why he never accepted any proposals. By the time the case came to court Ben's company was in receivership and the offers for settlement Joyce had previously refused looked very favourable compared to what she actually received.

Many men worry that they will be taken to the cleaners by their wives and that unrealistic orders will be made against them. This rarely happens in practice: a judge will look to see what money is available to support both parties. No one is going to be ruined, but the standard of living will have to drop for both parties – unless they are very wealthy.

Christopher still does not understand – even five years after his divorce – why his former wife Isobel did so well out of the divorce. He bought their flat himself which, as he prospered, they sold and moved on to one house and then another. When they divorced, she received over two-thirds of the capital in order to re-house herself and their children. Christopher still complains that Isobel ruined him, that she was excessively greedy, and that the law is completely unfair. Husbands like Christopher would do better to argue that their children 'ruined' them. Remember, it is always the children's need that come first.

Many wives conceal the fact that they have managed to find a small part-time job because they fear it will jeopardize their financial settlement. If the job is lowly and not well paid and the husband has a good salary it is unlikely to make much difference. The woman might argue that she has taken the job to give her an interest, and that the chance to meet people is more important to her than the money – but if this is the case, concealing the job could be misconstrued.

If, on the other hand, the job is well paid and has long-term prospects, a woman should nevertheless declare it. She will be penalized more if the job is discovered by accident.

Women, justifiably, are concerned that they may lose some of their entitlement if they become close to a man during divorce proceedings, particularly when their husband is about to remarry and has to support two households. Most men hope that their former wives will remarry; it could save them a great deal of money and leave them free from guilt, if they believe their wives will be happier.

A woman should think hard about concealing a new relationship. If she can prove that there is no likelihood of her marrying the man and that she still needs to be housed and have maintenance, it makes more sense to tell her solicitors so that her husband cannot use the information against her at a later date to seek to have the agreement order set aside for misrepresentation. The presence of a man might well affect the chances of a woman being given a huge lump sum settlement but, unless the relationship develops into something more permanent, it will do little for the size of her maintenance.

CHILDREN

Many people try various tactical moves during divorce proceedings, in order to get some apparent advantage, but these tactics tend to rebound, particularly when it comes to children. A judge will make a decision on what is in the best interests of the children, and will look through any tactical moves.

Graham did not really want to look after his children, but he was spiteful and wanted to make his wife, Nina, suffer as much as possible. He painted a most unflattering picture of her to the judge: he claimed that she was mentally unbalanced, that she was unable to look after the children properly because her own mother was an alcoholic and she had a sister who suffered from schizophrenia. Nina admitted that she was often distraught at home, but Graham was a bully and she had felt overwhelmed by him (mental cruelty had been cited in the divorce proceedings).

After the court had made enquiries into the family the judge, who did not believe that Nina would be unable to cope without Graham being there, ruled in her favour. There was no question that the children were extremely fond of her and did not see her as an imbecile.

On the other side of the same coin are those mothers who are convinced that their former husbands are louts and completely incapable of looking after the children and who, therefore, try to block the fathers' access. Karen was in this category, and had complained and nagged Stuart for most of their married life. She claimed that he did nothing for the children and was remote and not interested in them. The truth, which was rather painful for Karen to take on board, was that she had never allowed him to do anything with the children.

Almost immediately after their first child was born, Karen had chided Stuart for not doing things properly – from soothing the baby to changing a nappy. Over time, as what he did was always wrong in Karen's eyes, he gave up bothering. The judge in this case pointed out that his interest in the children was probably equal to the interest shown by many other fathers in happy marriages. Once he had the children on his own he would easily be able to look after them.

Many wives try to prevent their former husbands seeing their children if the 'other woman' is around. It is not possible to prevent this unless there are very exceptional circumstances, for example if the woman is a drug-pusher. Even to think there is some chance of being able to block the children's contact with their father is counter-productive. It is damaging to the children to give them any idea that they might not be able to see their father – they may agree to this suggestion just to keep their mother happy – and it means that the children's mother prefers them to suffer on her behalf. She takes it out on both her children and her husband: blocking access is the only way she can get back at him.

GENUINE CONCERNS

There are, of course, many situations where one party is concerned that his or her behaviour in the marriage will have some bearing on the financial settlement received or the proposed arrangements for the children.

Often, but not always, this will have been mentioned in the divorce petition and then repeated in the offer of financial settlement. For example, an extravagant wife who continued her high spending despite repeated warnings from her husband that he could not afford to support her, could well end up with a minimum settlement. But the husband cannot expect her to lose the children in these circumstances and cease to be their primary carer: an extravagant woman is not necessarily a bad mother. However, unreasonable behaviour that caused the children to suffer, for example, may affect a parent's chances of being able to see them. Mercifully these cases are rare.

Coming face-to-face with our imperfections is an uncomfortable process, and many people will try to avoid it. People who do not try to understand why their marriage has really failed, why the settlement is as fair as can be expected, or why they cannot see their children as often as they would wish are doomed to a miserable and bitter future. They will continue to hold their misapprehensions about their divorce as the only way of coping.

14

$\mathscr{A}$PPEARING IN COURT

One of the intimidating aspects of divorce is that it can involve courts
and judges, and for most people that conjures up a picture of a criminal
case and the panoply of a wigged judge and a jury.

But the divorce court, for the vast majority of cases, could not be less
like that. Only a handful of cases are held in open court where press
and public may attend: the divorce petitioned by actress Jenny Seagrove,
for example, was defended by her husband and was therefore heard
in open court. Not surprisingly, when either party is well known the case
creates considerable popular interest. As we pointed out in Chapter 5,
however, most cases are undefended and are 'heard' on paper.

In this chapter we shall look at the circumstances that may require
you to appear in court during or after your divorce, how to choose your
barrister, and what you should wear and how you should behave in
court. We also discuss whether or not you can be taken by surprise in
court.

APPEARING IN COURT DURING A DIVORCE

Judge not satisfied by the affidavit
There are a tiny number of cases when a district judge refuses to grant
the divorce and then the petitioner will have to appear in court and answer
various questions to satisfy the judge that the divorce should go ahead.

The judge may think, for example, that the allegations of unreasonable
behaviour made in the affidavit are not sufficiently strong on paper for
divorce to be granted, and so he or she will want to ask more questions.
A marriage, after all, is a legal contract and the judge, who has the
responsibility for terminating that contract, has to be satisfied that there
are real grounds (as required by the Matrimonial Causes Act) for the
divorce to be granted.

You will remember from Chapter 5 that your petition is supported by
an affidavit, the contents of which have to be true. If your petition was

properly drafted you will have few problems; sometimes the judge may say it is far too woolly and will return it for further explanation as he or she has to be satisfied that the petitioner is entitled to a divorce on the evidence presented.

Defended divorces

Defended divorces are so rare that we will only mention them briefly. Many people will be put off by the high costs because a defended divorce will always have a full hearing in court.

One way round a fully-defended divorce petition is for the aggrieved respondent to file an 'answer', which does not necessarily dispute all the allegations, and to ask for a divorce him- or herself on new grounds. This is called a cross-petition. Normally, the respondent's cross-petition then becomes the grounds for divorce.

It is unusual, but possible, to obtain cross-decrees: by the petitioner on the basis of his or her petition and the spouse on the basis of his or her cross-petition. This is obviously more expensive than a simple undefended petition, but is less costly and traumatic than a fully-defended divorce.

Defended divorces are inevitably doomed to fail because the party who wants the divorce will eventually be granted one, once the couple have lived apart for five years.

Defending a divorce is an expensive luxury and will only be undertaken by somebody who wants to make a fine legal point, has deep religious beliefs or has emotional and psychological problems coming to terms with the failure of the marriage. Ultimately, victory at defending a divorce is a Pyrrhic one, as the victor is left with a spouse who by definition wants the marriage to end.

One defended divorce arose because the petitioner cited the adultery of his spouse. His wife would not admit the adultery so there was a factual dispute over whether or not she had been unfaithful. This particular man, who wanted a speedy divorce in order to marry someone else, was unable to cite any other grounds for divorce – apart from admitting that he no longer loved his wife nor wanted to live with her.

Another husband chose to defend his wife's petition because he found it impossible to accept that the relationship had broken down irretrievably. Faced with the prospect of a long trial (after spending a morning in court), he accepted that little would be served by his defence and withdrew. He initially hoped for a reconciliation, but eventually had to accept that his marriage was over.

It is difficult for everyone when the respondent cannot accept the reality of his or her situation. 'There is nothing we can do to help those people, they must be allowed to have their say in court, if that is what they want and are prepared to pay for it. But it is a reminder not to use the legal process to work out the emotional problems of your marriage', comments one barrister.

Children's appointment

The most common reason for a person to appear in court during divorce proceedings is when a parent has to satisfy a judge that the arrangements made for the children are in their best interests. This is called either the children's appointment or the Section 41 appointment because it relates to the powers that a judge may exercise under Section 41 of the Matrimonial Causes Act 1973. There will only be an appointment if for some reason the judge is not satisfied with the proposed arrangements for the children. Since the implementation of the Children Act 1989, these appointments are no longer compulsory. If there is one, it will usually be on the same day that decree nisi is pronounced.

If there is an appointment, the petitioner must go to the appointment (the respondent must also go if the children will be living with him or her). Frankly, it is always sensible for both parents to go so that if the judge has any queries they can be dealt with instantly. Your children will not have to attend, and it is unusual (and could be a waste of money) for your solicitor to accompany you.

You will need to take a copy of the petition and a written statement of the proposed arrangements you have made on behalf of your children, and any other related documents, say, for example, when there have been other court orders concerning your children.

Unresolved disputes over money and children

Remember that only a tiny proportion of cases end up in court – you can sometimes gauge how good your solicitor is by knowing how few of his or her cases are disputed! When parents are at loggerheads over their children, the judge may recommend that each parent files an affidavit about what he or she thinks is best for the children, consult the in-court conciliation service, or may recommend that a court welfare officer prepares a report.

In these circumstances, both parties will eventually have to appear before a judge. It is up to either the father or mother to apply for a separate hearing date. These hearings are inevitably costly, both financially and emotionally, because it is advisable to take your solicitor and a barrister to argue your case for you.

Affidavits will have to be filed, and both parents and children will be interviewed by the court welfare officer. A decree nisi will not be granted until the court is satisfied that the children's best interests are being served.

This is not the case with money arrangements. Decree absolute can be granted even when a couple's finances are in a shambles. When there are court hearings over money, both parties, plus legal representatives, will attend.

APPEARING IN COURT AFTER DIVORCE PROCEEDINGS

An application to court to have the spouse's maintenance varied can take place at any time, provided the beneficiary has not remarried. Parents can apply for variations on behalf of their children until they are 18 or have finished full-time education, and again, they can do this at any time.

CHOOSING THE RIGHT BARRISTER

When you are summoned to appear before a judge – except for Section 41 appointments – you are likely to be represented either by a solicitor or a barrister.

It is just as important to be happy with your barrister as with your solicitor, so make sure you are confident that you have one sympathetic to your case. Your solicitor will recommend one for you, but if you do not like him or her, say so. Make sure that the barrister regularly deals with divorces and is not handling your case just as a favour for your solicitor.

In divorce cases barristers cannot afford to be as abrasive as, say, those working on commercial cases; they have to have the right sort of manner and sometimes be prepared to sit down with a client over lunch and work out what they should do – almost working as a social worker.

Good solicitors will not go to a barrister – however able that barrister may be – if he or she is always upsetting clients.

WHAT TO WEAR AND HOW TO BEHAVE

You are likely to be nervous before you see the judge and find the whole business completely terrifying, possibly the most nerve-wracking experience you have had since the marriage ceremony itself!

Rest assured that the judge will not bite your head off – he or she is human and has to listen to your evidence in order to decide what should be done. Except when a divorce is heard in open court – and this may happen when the circumstances are so unusual that they are thought to be in the public's interest and should be given wide coverage (and therefore there has to be enough space for journalists and spectators) – divorce courts will simply be a room 'in chambers'. The judge will sit behind a desk in normal everyday clothes, not wigged or robed, and there will be enough space for you, your spouse and your legal representatives.

One barrister who handles many divorce cases believes that women should dress respectably. Fashion aside, it is better not to wear a very short skirt or to be too flashy – it is unlikely to influence the judge in your favour; although you will not gain anything by being too formal.

Some women do try to influence judges by what they wear, particularly in financial applications. It does not make any sense for a woman to go along to court dressed smartly but claiming she is poor. If you have only one smart item that usually only appears at weddings, leave it in your wardrobe. If you wear it to court it will create the wrong impression. Similarly, if you are rich, do not dress in rags. It is much better for your clothes to reflect the way you live. One woman ignoring her solicitor's advice dressed very seductively to give her evidence, only to find that the judge's list had been changed and she was appearing before one of the female judges!

Women can afford to be more informal than men. Few judges would be impressed by a man who did not wear a jacket and tie, although a suit is not necessary. Do not forget that appearing in court is a serious business: a pullover would not be appropriate, any more than it was when you married. But if you never wear a jacket do warn your barrister and follow his or her advice.

Most people do not know how to address people in court. Magistrates and district judges are Sir or Madam. Circuit judges should be addressed as Your Honour, while a High Court judge is My Lord or My Lady. When you are attending a Section 41 appointment and you are not accompanied by a solicitor, make sure you know how to address the judge correctly.

The judge will ask whatever questions he or she wants. In addition, when you are represented your solicitor may ask questions, but you should always turn to the judge and direct your answers to him or her. This is, of course, completely unnatural, but try to take it in your stride. Speak up and do not go too fast, as the judge will be trying to absorb all you say, and will almost certainly be taking notes.

In financial relief cases, when a wife has no money, it is important that she creates the right impression on the judge because all she can do is describe her needs. It is important that the judge likes you and has sympathy with your case – but no more. So do not attempt to impress by being simpering or unctuous. If you become argumentative or rattle on too much you will irritate the judge. Be truthful (you are under oath) and natural and just try to answer the questions concisely and to the point.

This is all easier said than done when you are not used to doing it and when the atmosphere is emotionally so charged. Barristers and solicitors do not underestimate how difficult it can be.

We will never know if a performance effects the outcome, but judges (under those wigs, if worn) are human; they have been barristers or solicitors themselves and may even have been through their own divorce. A woman who is sharp and sarcastic and snipes at her husband may not be doing herself any favours – however bitter she feels. When judges give the reasons for their decisions, you do not know the unsaid and unconscious factors not spelled out in their judgements that they have taken into account.

No two people are going to behave in exactly the same way. Some people are resigned about the process, they are co-operative and any recriminations are left outside the court. Of course, it may be difficult to disguise your feelings if you are a young wife who has been left with three young children and your husband has gone off with your best friend!

Many people may find the process so overwhelming that they start to argue with the judge. It may be to your spouse's advantage for the judge to see you becoming annoyed. Your spouse may want to show that you are a person with a violent temper, so he or she will instruct his or her counsel to needle you. Equally, some people are naturally argumentative – but try not to respond aggressively or sarcastically to any of the questions, whoever asks them, and avoid passing any gratuitous opinions.

Your solicitor or barrister is there to argue on your behalf; you are there to give evidence. You must remember that this may be the first time you have seen your estranged spouse for some months and you may find it difficult to handle. So if you have a volatile temper try to restrain yourself, however angry your spouse makes you.

Violent scenes in court are not completely unknown: one barrister says he once saw a wife throttle her husband in the Court of Appeal, and on another occasion a man produced a dog chain in court and started threatening his wife and counsel.

Practise beforehand

You should always have a dry run with your solicitor. You should know exactly the type of questions the barrister is likely to ask you in court. Although your solicitor will have no way of knowing what questions the judge will ask, he or she should be able to give you a good idea of what will be covered.

CAN YOU BE TAKEN BY SURPRISE IN COURT?

In theory, your spouse and his or her barrister should not spring evidence on you because it should all have been disclosed beforehand, but sometimes a court appearance will reveal some unexpected information.

A man may have said in his affidavit that he had no Swiss bank account, then at court his wife produces a copy of one of the statements. Strictly this information should have been disclosed beforehand, but she and her solicitor may have wanted to secure the maximum advantage so they produce it during the proceedings. In these circumstances the woman would benefit because the man had been shown to be a liar and a perjurer.

A common trap is when one party discovers that his or her spouse has not been honest and therefore may be tempted not to be honest him- or herself. It is much more important to keep the moral advantage by being above reproach – you found your spouse to be dishonest, he or she is just as likely to find that you have been, too.

A surprising number of women are reluctant to tell the whole truth about a new relationship – possibly because they are frightened, or because they are worried that it is going to affect their financial entitlement or care of their children. While this can be true, it is not necessarily so. If you genuinely know it will not be a permanent relationship it is much better to tell your solicitor about it so that the information can be used to your benefit. When you deny any relationship and your spouse has suspicions and he is advised to employ a private detective to tail you, your case will look rather weak if the evidence is suddenly presented in court, even though, strictly, it should have been disclosed beforehand.

Some women do not disclose a part-time job when they should. Since their earning capacity is likely to be a factor in the level of maintenance they are awarded, their husbands may have discovered that they have found recent employment and, awkwardly but effectively, mention this in court.

Women who have been out of the job market for some years will find it difficult to find any work, and while a husband's solicitor will argue that the wife has a theoretical earning capacity the level is often unrealistic. While it is understandable that a wife may be tempted to hide the fact that she has a job, it is not recommended. Dishonesty will usually be found out.

15

$\mathscr{L}$EGAL COSTS – AND WHO FOOTS THE BILL?

Divorce can be expensive. A couple who end up fighting in court over their possessions and their children may end up spending £20,000 to £50,000 between them before they reach a settlement. And while both sides' honour may have been satisfied by the experience, that money will still have to come from their joint assets.

In other words, you have either to be wealthy enough for that sort of sum not to make any difference to your future lifestyle, or to believe that you will make gains (in terms of either money, more time with your children, or some material or emotional advantage) that outweigh the costs, had you decided not to fight.

We will explain later in this chapter the way that costs are apportioned, but you must always remember that even if your spouse has to pay a significant proportion of your costs, the money still has to come from your joint pool and the more you fight, the smaller the pool.

HOW ARE LAWYERS' FEES CALCULATED?

Solicitors charge by the hour. That means that every time you call him or her, every time a letter is written on your behalf, every time your solicitor contacts your spouse's solicitor and the time a junior solicitor spends taking your papers to and from court, are all charged to you. The minutes are all added together.

Hourly rates differ between firms of solicitors and also within firms. So if, for example, you consult someone at the top end of the scale, say the senior partner of an established London firm, you might have to pay £275 an hour (plus VAT). If you use one of the firm's junior solicitors, the charge might be £100 an hour. The senior partner of a reputable firm in a provincial town might charge £150 while junior staff in that same firm might charge £60.

Do not necessarily think that by using a solicitor who charges you £70 an hour rather than £120 per hour you will be given value for money.

The more expensive solicitor might be more experienced in matrimonial matters and give you better advice, so that your divorce goes through smoothly and with minimal fuss and in less time. The less experienced solicitor could inadvertently give you some poor advice which antagonizes your spouse so that you end up having to spend more time (and therefore money) sorting out the problem.

And do not necessarily think that if you are recommended an aggressive solicitor, because you think that it is the only way you will receive a fair deal from your spouse, that you will necessarily 'win'. An aggressive solicitor may win your case for you, but no solicitor is infallible, whatever his or her reputation. Ultimately you are at the mercy of the court, and some judges take a dim view of threatening tactics. Also, if you choose an aggressive firm, legal fees are likely to be higher than average. If you lose you are likely to lose heavily because the chances are that you will have incurred vast costs on the way. Beware, as solicitors make more money personally by taking cases to court (and cases that go to court take longer). An aggressive solicitor is more likely to fall into this category. At the end of the day, the fees on both sides come out of the common pot.

Judy, however, whose husband left her for a younger woman, was prepared for her solicitor to be aggressive. She announced to her solicitor: 'I really want to take him to the cleaners. I really want to get him', which she did. She was awarded a large chunk of his fortune which she knew would hurt him, but no more than the amount he should have offered her had he been advised properly and listened to that advice.

So there is no one answer to the question 'How much will the divorce cost?' When proceedings are straightforward, and there are no arguments over property or children, a divorce could cost as little as £300 or as much as £2,000, depending on the solicitor you use. As soon as you start arguing, the costs rise.

CAN I ASK HOW MUCH MY SOLICITOR WILL CHARGE?

You must *always* ask how much your solicitor charges, preferably the first time you meet: indeed, your solicitor is under an obligation to disclose this to you. If you feel intimidated, you should consider consulting a different solicitor. There may be times during your divorce that you have to ask the solicitor not to take certain action, and you must be completely comfortable when making difficult decisions or asking awkward questions.

You should ask what the solicitor thinks the total costs, roughly, of the divorce will be. You should make sure that you understand what share of the costs are likely to be yours. If your case is complicated or problematical the solicitor should give you an idea of the average costs of cases like yours to that particular firm. You should also find out whether the solicitor's fees include an additional percentage for 'care and attention' if your case has to be dealt with swiftly or if it is likely to be highly complicated, or whether 'care and attention' will be levied as an additional percentage at the end of proceedings.

You should ask for regular notification of the charges to date. This will give you an idea of how the hours tick by and also give you some warning if the costs are mounting out of control.

GOING TO COURT

When your divorce ends up in court, the costs do spiral out of control. For example, if both you and your spouse brief a barrister and the case lasts for a couple of days, your proceedings could cost over £50,000 per side. Settling out of court will save a great deal of money because barristers' fees tend to start in the thousands and preparation for trial is a time-consuming process.

It is always a bit of a lottery when a case goes to court, because so much depends on what impression your case makes on the judge who is trying your case. One case may settle easily, another may go on forever. Marion's and Daniel's case was the ultimate in expense. It revolved round the size of Daniel's pension, which Marion claimed made Daniel worth over £2 million, although he disputed the figure.

Marion obtained an accountant's report, and on the strength of that decided to sack her original solicitors and give her case to a more aggressive firm. This prompted Daniel to sack his own solicitor and also go to a fighter. They ended up battling up in court; a compromise was struck but they spent over £80,000 in legal costs.

HOW ARE COSTS APPORTIONED?

Both you and your spouse will be charged by your respective solicitors for their time, but once proceedings are under way there are ways of minimizing the chances of having to pay some of your spouse's costs as well as your own.

- If you are the petitioner, you can ask for the costs of obtaining the divorce decree (although costs are unlikely to be awarded to you when the petition is based on two years' separation with consent or five years' separation).

- In cases where adultery and unreasonable behaviour are cited the respondent (and co-respondent, if relevant) usually have to pay the costs of the divorce. In a sense, therefore, the courts do recognize some blame attached to the respondent – although this is not reflected in the way the assets will be apportioned.

- If you have to take out an injunction against your spouse during divorce proceedings you can, theoretically, apply for costs. But you may not obtain them if, for example, your spouse should disappear or turn out to have no funds him- or herself. Do not forget you are primarily liable to your solicitor for your own costs.

- When there is a battle over children, the fact that a residence order is made deciding where the children should live does not mean that the other parent will have to pay costs. Both parents are likely to have to foot their own bills. The court is only likely to order one parent to pay the other's costs if that parent has been unreasonable during proceedings.

- When a woman is granted maintenance, or allowed to stay living in the family home, she cannot necessarily expect costs to be awarded to her, even if she has no assets herself, unless her husband has steadfastly refused to make a reasonable offer. However, when the maintenance is awarded the court is likely to include a sum to cover her legal expenses.

- You should make a request 'for costs' at each stage of the proceedings if you want your spouse to pay part of your legal costs out of his or her share of your joint assets. This is not just when you are dealing with the divorce proceedings, but also when you are dealing with any related matters such as your house or maintenance. Although the decision on costs will be deferred until the final hearing of your case, you must request them continually. At the final hearing, the court will be aware that the spouse who has requested costs will still have to meet some of the overall bill, because even when costs are awarded, they are usually for only between 60 and 80 per cent of the actual bill charged by the solicitor. In such cases, the settlement awarded to the petitioner might be increased to cover the costs.

Christine was involved in a straightforward divorce and had costs of £225 awarded to her. Her total bill was over £1,000 because she was a demanding client and rang her solicitor unreasonably often; thus she had to pay the difference herself.

A CALDERBANK LETTER

One way of speeding up proceedings and keeping costs under control is to send your spouse's solicitor a 'without prejudice' offer, setting out the terms on which you would be willing to settle your case and reserving the right to refer to it when judgement has been given on the question of costs. This offer, known as a Calderbank letter (from the name of the case which set the precedent) means that if your spouse is not willing to accept the terms and you become involved in protracted negotiations or even end up in court the details of the offer will be made known to the judge at the end of proceedings.

If the judge grants your spouse less than the terms you have offered, your spouse may have to pay both sets of costs from the date the offer was made. If you are sent a Calderbank letter, you have a duty to respond to it if you believe the terms are unfair, stating what you are prepared to settle for. If you do not, you may be penalized for your failure to do so.

You will appreciate how you can speed proceedings up by concentrating your spouse's intentions, and simply sending a Calderbank letter, provided your offer is reasonable and if you have given full disclosure of your means. Your spouse's solicitor is likely to advise his or her client to settle on the terms suggested in the letter if they are generous enough, because otherwise your spouse runs the risk of having to pay all the costs run up on both sides from the moment the letter was received.

In fact, fewer than 10 per cent of financial applications ever reach a full court hearing, although quite a large proportion are settled just before the date of the hearing.

HOW ARE COSTS CALCULATED AND AWARDED?

Taxation

This is the process in which the district judge or taxing officer at a court examines the solicitor's files and bill in detail and works out whether the charges are reasonable, bearing in mind the simplicity or complexity of your case. Your solicitor must give a comprehensive breakdown of all the steps taken during your divorce proceedings, detailing the charges of all stages.

This process is used in two instances:

- When you query the size of your solicitor's bill at the end of your divorce proceedings. You should start the process within a month of the date of the bill.
- If your spouse is awarded costs against you, your solicitor will want to know how the figure was reached before agreeing that you should pay, and may want your spouse's solicitor's bill to be taxed by the court. There is a procedure set out in the Matrimonial Causes (Costs) Rules to help the taxing officer determine what costs are reasonable.

For privately funded litigation, and also when a client is legally-aided, there are rules and regulations limiting the rates for, say, answering a letter and preparing documents.

OTHER COSTS

There are fixed court fees that have to be paid during proceedings, which include the fees when the petition is submitted, when the petitioner asks for the court to make the decree absolute, and when either side applies for ancillary relief (maintenance and/or lump sum payments) or at any particular stage of the action (for instance if you have to ask the court to get your spouse to file his or her affidavit). These fees are not particularly expensive in the context of your entire bill, the most common ones being only £10.

When calculating costs of divorce, remember that they may include the cost of house sales and purchases, and all the attendant legal and surveyors' fees and Stamp Duty. And if your finances are particularly complicated and involved – say, in a family business – your solicitor may recommend that you appoint an accountant to report on the business, and that will obviously be an additional cost which could run into thousands.

KEEPING COSTS DOWN

- Try to be efficient during proceedings. Keep all your documents, papers and letters together. When your solicitor asks for information, answer all the questions in detail and promptly. Do not waste time (and money) by having to be chased up by your solicitor.

- If at all possible come to some agreement with your spouse, without involving solicitors. The more your can decide yourselves, the more money there will be to share between you.
- Only use your solicitor for strictly legal advice (see Chapter 4).
- Only be prepared to fight if you really believe that you are going to make considerable gains.

Jessica, for example, was sure that her screenwriter husband had not declared all his freelance earnings for the two years before they separated – possibly by as much as £20,000. Her solicitor advised her not to demand that he disclose further details on the grounds that his existing offer to her was reasonable, that it might cost her over £1,000 in legal fees to chase for the disclosure, and, in the end, she would be lucky to receive as much as an extra £5,000. She would also run the risk of ruining any potentially reasonable relationship with her former husband.

Florence was successful in obtaining an order that her husband Gavin pay her legal costs. After the proceedings and before the costs were paid, however, Gavin went bankrupt. Florence was obliged to meet her solicitor's costs. Furthermore, should she have wished to do so, she would then have had to incur further expenses employing her solicitor to try to recover the costs in the bankruptcy hearings.

16

$\mathscr{A}$RE YOU ENTITLED TO LEGAL AID?

When you first go and visit a solicitor you should, as we explained in Chapter 15, discuss how much he or she charges. All solicitors are obliged to tell you whether or not you are entitled to what is loosely called legal aid. If you could claim and you are not made fully aware of this, and your solicitor charges you privately, he or she will have to forfeit the fees when your divorce becomes absolute and your financial affairs are settled. (See Chapter 3, page 22 on how to complain about your solicitor).

There is one disadvantage of using the legal aid scheme. Some specialist divorce solicitors do not handle legal aid work, so you may have to work a bit harder to find a solicitor who does. One barrister who spends most of his time dealing with family matters candidly said that not all solicitors handling divorces under the legal aid scheme are up to date, and do not always give their clients the best advice. This is not because they are not intelligent, or good solicitors; it is simply because they are not specialists. There are a number of solicitors who handle legal aid work and are specialists – it is worth asking around.

Barbara, for example, was in her late forties. She had not worked during her 20-year marriage (except for a few months before she became pregnant with her first child) and had no capital of her own. Although her husband was wealthy, she was entitled to legal aid. In spite of this she decided to consult a matrimonial specialist who did not take on legal aid work, knowing that she would have to pay her share of the legal costs at the end of the proceedings. Moreover, even if she had used the legal aid scheme she would eventually have had to contribute towards her costs, although they would have been lower than the bill she did in fact have to pay.

Julia, on the other hand, who was in her thirties, had a rather more tricky decision to make. She and her husband Tim had been given a large but run-down house after the death of an aunt. It was in Tim's name alone, although they had been living there for 15 years. Neither of them had any other money and they were both entitled to legal aid. But Tim was a bully and Julia knew that she might easily be railroaded into an unfavourable settlement. So she decided to use an experienced solicitor who was recommended to her but who did not work under the legal aid scheme. Not unexpectedly, Tim turned out to be difficult and, by the time proceedings came to an end, the costs for Julia were £3,000. While many people might consider this a complete waste of money, Julia was satisfied. She argued that had she not been able to trust her solicitor to argue to the bitter end on her behalf she might not have received such a decent settlement and she might have been at least £6,000 less well off. In addition, she knew that, finally, she had not succumbed to Tim's bullying.

The grim truth about divorce is that people with few assets, and a little capital tied up in a property, are likely to have to spend a larger proportion of that money in legal fees than either the rich or the poor. When you have a great deal of money or no money there is less room for argument.

In 1990–91, nearly 138,000 legal aid certificates were issued by the Legal Aid Board for matrimonial cases. It is difficult to say how many divorces that covers, because in some cases only one party will be granted legal aid, but it could be between 80,000 and 100,000 divorces – the majority of all divorce cases over that period.

WHAT IS LEGAL AID?

'Legal aid' is a term used loosely to cover both legal advice and assistance and legal aid. A booklet called *A Practical Guide to Legal Aid* is available free of charge from The Legal Aid Board (address in Appendix C); it gives you a comprehensive guide to claiming. People in Scotland should write to The Scottish Legal Aid Board (address in Appendix C), and those in Northern Ireland should contact the Incorporated Law Society of Northern Ireland (address in Appendix C). We have outlined what is meant by legal aid below.

LEGAL ADVICE AND ASSISTANCE

Legal advice and assistance – also known as the green form scheme (because of the colour of the application form) – means that, provided you are financially eligible, legal advice and assistance will be given free of charge or for a contribution towards the costs (depending on your circumstances): in general terms this covers work normally done for you in an office.

Under this scheme your solicitor can give you advice, make telephone calls for you and deal with your correspondence, but will not be able to appear in court on your behalf. You may be able to apply for extra help under this scheme and, for proceedings in the Family Proceedings (Magistrates') Court, you could be given 'assistance by way of representation' (ABWOR). This means your solicitor may be able to apply on your behalf in a magistrates' court for maintenance before divorce proceedings get going.

The financial limits for legal advice and assistance and legal aid schemes are re-assessed each year, and the new figures come into effect at the beginning of April each year. Your solicitor should have these figures to hand but, if not, your local Citizens Advice Bureau can help, or your local Legal Aid Board (both listed in the telephone directory). Table 2 on pages 130–31 show the figures as of April 1992.

Are you entitled to legal advice and assistance?
Whether or not you can make a claim depends on a number of factors: your savings and other capital, your weekly income, your outgoings and the number of people, including children, dependent on you.

Capital
Your family home and its contents, including personal possessions, are not included in this assessment. However, your shares and savings must not be more than a certain figure, which is graded according to the number of dependants you have.

Disposable income
Your weekly disposable income is limited as well if you hope to have legal advice and assistance. This is not simply your take-home pay. In addition to deductions for tax and National Insurance contributions, you deduct an allowance for your spouse and children and if, at the end of that exercise, you have less than the maximum permitted, you are entitled to legal advice. You will be assessed independently, however wealthy your spouse is, if your spouse has opposing interests to you, or you are not living together. That means you may still be under the

same roof, but because you are seeking advice on divorce, your interests are conflicting.

Income support
If you receive income support, family credit or disability working allowance you are automatically entitled to free legal advice and assistance, provided you do not exceed the savings threshold. Those receiving income support are also entitled to ABWOR (subject only to the merits test).

Contribution
Even when your weekly disposable income is below the income limit you may have to make some contributions towards your legal fees. Below a certain level you will receive your legal advice completely free; between the two figures you may have to make some contribution. However, you will probably find it is worth paying this small contribution because you will be exempt from some court fees; if you were to pay privately the fees would be much higher.

Entitlements under the green form scheme
The scheme entitles you to 3 hours (or 2 hours if you are a respondent, if no petition is drafted) of your solicitor's time, covering the following areas:

- general advice on whether or not you have grounds for divorce
- how you go about obtaining a divorce
- drafting the petition and drawing up the affidavit
- advising you about what action to take, if you are the respondent
- advice on obtaining an injunction
- registration of a land charge on your home
- advice about arrangements you can make for children
- advice about maintenance for you and/or your spouse and children
- helping you decide where you are to live
- dealing with correspondence from your spouse and his or her solicitor

When the initial time limit is used up, your solicitor can apply to the Legal Aid Board for extra hours. A request is usually granted if your solicitor can show that you need the extra time to sort out your affairs and that it would not be more appropriate to apply for civil aid.

You are entitled to only one green form for your divorce and associated proceedings, but you may be able to fill in another form and claim a further two hours' free advice if you have problems with debts or payments of, say, your electricity and gas bills, or you need advice on what benefits you may claim.

LEGAL AID

When you have been using the green form scheme and there are problems over, say, the arrangements for your children, your maintenance, or a lump sum you are expecting from your spouse, you can apply for legal aid. Legal aid is not available for uncontested divorces but Green Form advice is available. If your request is granted a certificate will be issued. This certificate means that your solicitor's and barrister's fees will be paid initially from the legal aid fund. If you have no assets and do not gain any by the end of all the proceedings all your fees will be paid from the legal aid fund (subject to any contribution you are liable to make). However, if you receive a lump sum, say, after the sale of the family home, your legal costs will be deducted from this sum before it is passed on to you. This deduction is used to pay the 'statutory charge' (see below).

The application forms are quite complicated but there are only two stages to the process: a means test and a merits test. You will have to give full details of your income and outgoings, your dependants and your savings. Your employer will also have to fill in a form confirming your income. If you are self-employed you have to fill in the same form, and provide details of your earnings backed up with copies of your accounts. There are different forms for those receiving income support or resident outside England and Wales.

The Legal Aid Board area office will examine your application to see whether or not it is justified, and the legal aid assessment officer at the Benefits Agency (formerly the Department of Social Security) has to assess what contribution you may have to make. It can take weeks before a certificate is issued, although an emergency certificate can be issued to cover the costs of any urgent work. This may mean that cases grind to a halt because a solicitor cannot claim fees for work done for you until the certificate is granted.

Are you entitled to legal aid?
Legal aid is means and merits tested and whether or not you qualify depends on how much disposable income and disposable capital you have (excluding your home). The limits are higher than under the green form scheme, but if either limit is exceeded you are ineligible for support. Husbands and wives are assessed separately.

As with the green form scheme you will have to make a contribution towards your legal costs unless your disposable income is very low. Table 2 (pages 130–31) gives the limits of capital and income, plus details of contributions you may have to make towards your costs.

If you have to contribute towards your legal aid, you are sent an offer giving you details of how much you will have to pay. Contributions based on income are usually paid in 12 monthly instalments. When a lump sum is requested you must pay it immediately. The legal aid certificate will not be issued until you have accepted the offer and paid the first of the monthly contributions and any lump sum. (Do remember that you will have to pay your solicitor for any work done on your behalf before the certificate is granted which is not covered by the green form scheme; although if the work comes under the green form criteria it is worth checking whether or not your solicitor has applied for a green form extension. Only if an extension is refused should your solicitor ask you to pay).

When your income changes
If your disposable income increases or decreases you must let the Legal Aid Board know. Similarly, if you receive a windfall and your disposable capital increases you must also let the Legal Aid Board know. You may either have to pay an amended contribution or the certificate may be taken away.

Topping up legal aid
This is strictly forbidden, however tempting. One of the disadvantages of using the legal aid system is that you will lose some control over what your solicitor can do for you. There are limits on what a solicitor can claim, and if your case is going to court and your solicitor believes you need to brief a barrister, your solicitor may decide to send a junior member of his or her firm to support you rather than go with you.

You cannot insist that your solicitor join you and it is strictly prohibited to offer more money for him or her to go with you.

THE STATUTORY CHARGE

While you may be entitled to legal aid during the proceedings, you may face 'a statutory charge' once the proceedings are concluded and you receive your share of the assets. When the legal aid fund pays out more than it collects in contributions from you and from any costs your spouse is ordered to pay, the legal aid fund has first bite of the cherry from money or property released or transferred to you. This charge covers all the legal proceedings relating to the divorce – not just those dealing with your property.

The statutory charge covers any lump sum payment you receive, the value of the house or flat (or your share of it) and any other asset that was either transferred between you and your spouse or kept by you as part of the divorce agreement. In matrimonial proceedings the first £2,500 of any property gained from your spouse or kept by you is exempt from the charge; neither does the charge apply to maintenance paid to wives or children.

The only circumstances when you would not have a statutory charge levied on your property would be when you and your spouse could demonstrate convincingly that the house was genuinely never in dispute. Ideally, if it could be done in time, you and your spouse should send an agreed statement with the application for legal aid, so that the Legal Aid Board would know from the start that neither of you stand to benefit financially from the proceedings.

If the property is being transferred to one legally-aided spouse – rather than sold – that spouse may not have to pay the statutory charge there and then. Instead, the charge may be put on the house but not be enforced until the house is sold.

For example, Theresa's certificate covered proceedings against her husband, a residence application for their two children, and an application for the family home to be transferred to her name. She was rather surprised to discover that the legal fees for all these proceedings would eventually have to be met when the house was sold, even if that were not until the children left home.

Jackie and Maurice were fighting over their house, which was in their joint names. Maurice had been out of work and unable to contribute much to the upkeep. Jackie did not lose her ownership of the house, but the statutory charge was still to be enforced once Jackie came to sell the house.

Whenever payment of the statutory charge to the Legal Aid Board is postponed, interest is levied from the date of registration of the charge until the date the charge is paid off. When eventually you pay the statutory charge you will have to pay the accumulated interest as well, so bear in mind that the amount you will eventually have to pay may be much higher than the original charge, so if you can pay it off more quickly, so much the better.

Couples with no assets and who, say, live in a council house will have all their legal fees paid for by the legal aid fund – even if they are arguing about which of them is going to get the tenancy of the house at the end of the proceedings.

But, remember, even when you are legally aided, it is easy to run up huge costs if you fight over petty details, or if you are not prepared to accept a reasonable offer from your spouse. You may even be reported to the Legal Aid Board by your spouse if your solicitor is being unnecessarily litigious. So keep a tab on your costs – you may well have to foot the bill at the end of proceedings.

Once your financial affairs have been sorted out and any payment (except maintenance) has come through, your solicitor will have to pay it into the legal aid fund – before you receive any money yourself. You then have to wait until the legal aid fund has settled up the costs before you are paid the balance.

If, however, your solicitor undertakes that his or her costs will not be more than a certain amount, he or she can just pay that amount into the fund so that the rest comes immediately to you. If the money is to be used to buy a new home, your solicitor will keep it for this purpose once the Legal Aid Board has agreed to defer payment of the charge; once your new house has been purchased the charge will be put on this new property.

Do you qualify for legal advice and assistance – the green form scheme?

SAVINGS:

Add up your savings. This includes the value of your savings, whether in cash, investments, money in a bank or the National Savings Bank and anything you own of substantial value, such as furs and jewellery. Leave out:

- The value of the house you live in
- Your household furniture and effects, clothing and any tools of your trade.
- The value of the thing that you want advice about. For instance if you are in dispute about who owns an antique clock, leave out its value.

The capital limit is:

£1000 if you have no dependants
£1335 if you have one dependant
£1535 if you have two dependants
£1635 if you have three dependants
£100 for each extra dependant

If your disposable capital exceeds this you will not be eligible.

INCOME

If you are receiving income support, family credit or disability working allowance you will be eligible for free legal advice and assistance unless your disposable capital exceeds the limit.

If you are not receiving income support, family credit or disability working allowance, your solicitor will take the actual income in the last seven days of yourself and your husband or wife and deduct from it:

i Income tax and National Insurance contributions.

ii £40.69 for your partner if you are living together whether or not there is a conflict of interest. Where you are separated or divorced deduct the actual maintenance paid by you in the past seven days.

iii The following allowances for children and dependants:
Dependent children and relatives

under 11	£18.19
between 11 and 15	£26.75
between 16 and 17	£31.94
18 and over	£42.00

There are built-in allowances for rent, rates, and other expenses. What is left after making these deductions is your disposable income. You qualify for legal advice and assistance if your disposable income is £145.00 per week or less and your disposable capital is below the capital limit. The capital limit for ABWOR is £3000 plus the same capital dependant's allowances as shown in the first column. All people receiving income support are eligible.

Do you qualify for legal aid?

SAVINGS

Add up your savings. These include:

- Cash savings, bank or National Savings Bank accounts, National Savings Certificates, Premium Savings Bonds.
- Money that can be borrowed against the surrender value of any life insurance or endowment policies.
- Anything you own of value, such as furs, jewellery, antiques, etc.
- The value of any dwelling other than that in which you live.

But leave out:

- The value of the house you live in.
- Your furniture and fittings, clothes and any tools of your trade.
- The value of the thing that your case is about. For instance, if you are in dispute about who owns an antique clock, leave out its value.

What is left after making these deductions is your *disposable capital*. If your *disposable capital* is £3000 or less you will qualify for legal aid.

If your *disposable capital* is £3000 or less, or if you are receiving income support, you will not have to pay a contribution. If your savings are more than £3000 and less than £6750 you will have to pay a contribution; this is likely to be required at once. The maximum you will be asked to pay is *all* your *disposable capital* over £3000.

The calculation of disposable capital is different for some pensioners. Men of 65 or over and women of 60 or over may benefit from an extra allowance.

If their annual disposable income is less than £3060 (excluding net income earned from capital) then certain amounts of savings are disregarded so that they can still qualify for Legal Aid despite their total savings being more than the usual capital limit.

The amounts that are disregarded are set out below. Remember this does only apply to pensioners on disposable incomes of less than £3060 excluding net income earned from capital. This means that capital which produces an income on which the applicant lives is not taken into account for assessing disposable income.

You must obtain a copy of A Practical Guide to Legal Aid from The Legal Aid Board, Fifth and Sixth Floors, 29/37 Red Lion Street, London WC1R 4PP. Tel 071 831 4209 for further details.

Annual disposable income (excluding net income capital)	Amount of capital disregarded
Up to – £350	£35,000
£351 – £800	£30,000
£801 – £1200	£25,000
£1201 – £1600	£20,000
£1601 – £2050	£15,000
£2051 – £2450	£10,000
£2451 – above	£5,000

INCOME

The assessment officer assesses your income for the following 12 months and deducts income tax, National Insurance, superannuation, pension contributions, employment expenses (i.e. fares to work, trade union membership and child care where reasonable), rent, water rates, community charge, mortgage payments and allowances for your family and dependants. The mobility component of the disability living allowance is disregarded.

The allowances for your family and dependants are:

	yearly
Partner	£2122

Dependent children and relatives:

Under 11	£948
Between 11 and 15	£1395
Between 16 and 17	£1665
18 and over	£2190

What is left is your *disposable income*. If it is £3060 or less per year, you will qualify on income.

If your *disposable income* is £3060 per year or less you pay no contribution. If it is between £3060 and £6800 you have to pay towards the cost of your case from your income. The contribution will be a quarter of the excess of your disposable income above £3060.

$\mathscr{C}$OHABITATION AND PRE-MARRIAGE CONTRACTS

This chapter looks at two seemingly unrelated topics: cohabitation and pre-marriage contracts. Of course they are completely different in substance, but they are similar in one crucial respect: namely that there are no laws of the stature of the divorce legislation to protect you if you are cohabiting, and a pre-marriage contract has no legal substance when it comes to divorce.

COHABITATION

It is estimated that about a million couples in England and Wales between the ages of 18 and 40 live together. While many of these couples do marry and have children, a significant proportion split up (some having had children) and find themselves in unexpected difficulties.

For a start, although while living as man and wife you may be dubbed 'common-law' husband and wife, the law, in fact, treats you almost as if you were strangers.

Secondly, when a cohabiting relationship breaks down, do not think you will be able to extricate yourself without any of the mess you commonly suppose surrounds divorce. When a man and woman have lived together for years, the chances are that their finances and other affairs have overlapped (they may, for example, both jointly own the flat they live in). Disentangling the finances and property and coming to some agreement can be even more complicated than for a divorcing couple simply because there is no legal framework to help the couple, or their solicitors, divide the spoils. All they can do is to look coldly at the financial contributions made by each party, and at the way in which property is legally held. However, if violence becomes an issue in the break-up of the relationship, cohabitees have similar protection to married couples, under the Domestic Violence and Matrimonial Proceedings Act.

Financial arrangements

When a marriage breaks down, the court makes sure that the couple's assets are distributed as fairly as possible – depending on the needs of the individuals and their dependants. But when the couple is not married, the court has no powers to decide on what constitutes a fair arrangement. It can only decide who actually owns a particular item (whether it is the flat or a painting) by finding out who bought it, whether it was a present or who made most contributions towards it.

Stephanie, for example, found that she had no financial claim on her home (although she had plenty of moral claim) even though she and Oliver had been living together for 12 years: her name was not on the title deeds. She was able to claim a small part of the capital because she could prove that she had contributed to the mortgage payments and helped pay some of the bills, but she did not receive the lump sum she could have expected had she and Oliver been married.

Ellen was in an even weaker position. She had sacrificed her own career to look after the two children she had with Kenneth, and so had made no financial contributions to the family, and thus no claim against the house. She found that she had no automatic right to stay in the house with the children. She could, however, make an application for maintenance and a lump sum and property transfer for the children (which would include housing provision) under the Children Act.

The length of the relationship and having helped to run a family business – two further factors that would very much count in the favour of a divorcing woman when capital is divided – are of no relevance when it comes to the break up of a cohabiting relationship.

Ellen's position became even bleaker. Much to her dismay, despite her devotion to the children she discovered that Kenneth had no obligations to provide her with any maintenance for herself. She had to fight him in court, on the grounds that because he did not want to look after the children himself, part of their maintenance had to include a sum for the child care which she provided.

Ironically, people who live together for years, have children, belatedly decide to marry and then find that the marriage is on the rocks and split up after a relatively short time, are at some advantage over couples who cohabit without ever getting married. They will find the length of time they spent cohabiting will be taken into account when they discuss the financial consequences of their separation. In reality the marriage might have only lasted 18 months, but the woman's solicitors would argue that her entitlement to capital and income is based on the entirety of their relationship, including the time spent cohabiting, say, eight or ten years.

Arrangements for children
Although a cohabiting woman may seem to be at a complete disadvantage financially, cohabiting fathers have to cope with lack of parental rights if the relationship fails. While a married couple has joint responsibility for the care and upbringing of their children, only the mother has these legal rights, unless she has agreed to let the father share potential responsibility, or unless the father has been awarded parental responsibility by the court. So she will choose the child's name, sign a consent form for any operations the child must undergo and decide what (if any) religion the child should observe.

An unmarried father does not even have 'automatic' parental responsibility or guardianship of the children if the mother dies, although of course he can make an application to look after the children if he wants to play a prominent role in their lives at that stage.

PRE-MARRIAGE CONTRACTS
There is a trend in the United States for couples on the point of marriage to draw up 'pre-nuptial' agreements on how they are going to live (sometimes covering even minor details such as who is going to do the washing-up and the shopping, or how many times a week each partner can go out alone in the evening) and how they would divide their property and other assets if they divorced.

In UK law, these pre-marital contracts have no legal standing – for a number of reasons:

- In the event of divorce, the legal framework already exists for dividing a couple's assets. While the contract could form the basis of discussions between husband and wife, the terms of the contract are not binding and cannot be upheld in a court of law – because the divorce proceedings take precedence.
- One party may decide that the terms of the contract are no longer in his or her interests – and there is nothing that the other party can do about this.

- Solicitors may advise a divorcing person to ignore the pre-marriage contract because the terms are unfair to their client.
- Circumstances can change during a marriage. For instance, the wife's needs may be greater than they were before the marriage (because she has children, for example, or because she has been stricken by an illness such as rheumatoid arthritis).

Erica was distraught that her husband, Douglas, had declared their pre-marriage contract null and void, and was angry that he had broken his word. She asked her solicitor for a court ruling on it, but the solicitor pointed out to her that the very fact that they were involved in a divorce meant that they had both broken their word (their marriage vows). The contract was valueless; the jurisdiction of the divorce court could not be ousted.

Fay and Nick were both happy to honour their pre-marriage contract and to take 50 per cent each of the value of the capital in their flat. However, after eight years of marriage, Nick was earning a much larger salary than Fay, even though when they had married they earned approximately the same.

Fay's solicitor persuaded her to argue for a much larger proportion of the capital as a lump sum settlement. Initially she was reluctant to do this, but eventually she accepted that because neither she nor Nick could have anticipated the difference that developed in their earning capacity when they drew up their pre-marriage contract: the contract had little relevance for their current financial position.

Had the contract been drawn up, say, after six years of marriage, Fay would have been less likely to accept such unfavourable terms. Her decision antagonized Nick but he, too, appreciated why their contract no longer had any validity.

18

*D*IVORCE IN NORTHERN IRELAND AND SCOTLAND; AND WHEN A DIVORCE SHOULD TAKE PLACE ABROAD

This handbook has concentrated on proceedings in England and Wales. In this chapter we will outline the procedure for people living in other parts of the United Kingdom, and look briefly at when you should consider divorce proceedings abroad.

NORTHERN IRELAND

Proceedings in Northern Ireland are for the most part similar to those in England and Wales, although there are some differences because the Matrimonial and Family Proceedings Act does not apply, although a similarly named order was passed in 1989. The main differences are as follows:

- A petition cannot be filed until two years after the marriage.
- Divorces do not take place on paper to the same extent. People involved in a divorce must go to the court themselves and give their evidence to a judge.
- Everyone, subject to means, can get legal aid for the divorce proceedings.

SCOTLAND

In Scotland things are strikingly different.

- You can start divorce proceedings under Scottish legislation if you or your spouse live in Scotland or were based there for at least a year immediately before you start proceedings.
- There is no minimum period after marriage before you can start proceedings.
- Grounds for divorce are similar to those under English and Welsh law, although if your spouse commits adultery you do not have to

demonstrate that you find it intolerable to live with him or her. However, if you continue to live with your spouse for more than three months after you first knew about the adultery, it can no longer be used as grounds.

- Divorces are dealt with either in sheriff courts or the Court of Session in Edinburgh.
- Decree nisi and decree absolute do not exist. The court grants a single decree of divorce which is immediately effective, although time is allowed for an appeal.

There are two forms of divorce procedure in Scotland. The d-i-y divorce and the ordinary procedure divorce.

The d-i-y divorce

This is the most straightforward form of divorce and can be done, as the name suggests, by yourself. You are eligible for this kind of divorce when you and your spouse have lived apart for either two or five years (depending on your circumstances), you have no children under the age of 16, there are no squabbles over money and neither of you has a history of psychiatric illness.

While you do not need a solicitor for this type of divorce (all you have to do is fill in some printed forms), it is worth obtaining some legal advice to make sure you are not losing out through ignorance.

Once you have filled in Part One of the form (and your spouse Part Two of the form, if you are divorcing after a two-year separation) you fill in Part Three – the affidavit – and swear it before a notary public (who is a solicitor and will charge you for the service) or a justice of the peace (whose services are free). You send the completed form along with your marriage certificate and payment for court fees to the court, and you will be notified when the divorce has been granted (usually within a couple of months).

Ordinary procedure

Ordinary procedure in many ways matches the English and Welsh variety, and because this kind of divorce is likely to be more complicated it is a good idea to have a solicitor. Legal advice and assistance are available under a pink form scheme and eligibility for this support, and legal aid, follows similar limits to those in England and Wales.

Initial writ

Proceedings start when your solicitor lodges an initial writ in court – like the petition in England and Wales. You are called the pursuer and your spouse the defender. As well as setting out the grounds for divorce you can apply for various interim orders which will stand until the divorce comes through and fresh orders are granted.

These orders cover:

• Money
• Custody and access to the children and orders preventing them being taken out of Scotland
• Orders preventing violent behaviour from your spouse and keeping your spouse out of the matrimonial home.

Divorces are not usually defended on the merits in Scotland (when the divorce is defended, the case is heard in court). More commonly, your spouse will defend your application for financial orders or apply for similar orders. When the arguments are only about money and/or children, the divorce proceedings themselves take place on paper although the court will hear evidence relating to your money and children. Your divorce decree will not be issued until these are sorted out.

Affidavits

These are equally important in Scotland as they are in England and Wales. In addition, if you and your spouse are in complete agreement on how the children are going to be looked after, you can put all this in a sworn affidavit (plus a testimony from a relative or friend of the family who sees the children regularly) and a judge will accept the arguments without seeing either of you or your children. When you cannot agree, the court asks for a report from an independent person – usually a lawyer, but sometimes a social worker.

Decree

The decree is the legal document containing the orders made by the court. The financial orders are usually granted at the same time as the divorce, although it is possible for these to be delayed if disagreement is holding up the divorce.

The court will let you know when the decree has been granted and will also let your spouse know, if his or her whereabouts are known. There is a 14-day period allowed for appeal. After that, an 'extract' (a certified copy) of the decree can be obtained which shows the details of the orders the court made. You will need an extract to show that you are divorced if you plan to marry again, and to enforce financial orders if your spouse refuses to pay.

Financial arrangements

If you and your spouse can agree on the financial arrangements – both for you and your children – you can submit a 'joint minute' to the court outlining the orders you both wish to be granted. The court will then normally grant them without further enquiry, so it is important for you to be satisfied with the details before the minute is submitted, because it will be difficult to change them at a later date.

When you and your spouse cannot come to any amicable agreement over money, you may submit further affidavits from both sides. These will state your income, capital and your living needs. Even then it is extremely rare for either of you to have to give evidence in person in court about your financial circumstances.

The sorts of financial arrangements made between a husband and wife are not that dissimilar to those in England and Wales. The types of arrangement are made under The Family Law (Scotland) Act 1985 which sets out a series of principles to guide the court when making its financial orders. The orders will include 'aliment' for the children. This is like maintenance and is awarded until the child reaches the age of 18. From then to age 25, aliment is payable if the child needs support because he or she is in some form of further education.

In general, exactly as in England and Wales, a lump sum settlement is once and for all. However, in Scotland there are two exceptions: if you or your spouse lied in order to obtain a certain sum, the court can make a new order; if your former spouse becomes bankrupt within five years and the order resulted in his or her debts exceeding assets, the court can order you to repay all or part of the lump sum. Otherwise all the court can do is to alter the way in which the lump sum is paid, perhaps by ordering payment by instalments or giving the relevant spouse more time to pay.

DIVORCE IN EIRE

Full divorce in Eire is not permitted. However, in 1989 the Judicial

Separation & Family Law Reform Act was passed and it is now possible for couples to apply for a judicial separation. In effect, this Act terminates the marriage relationship, allows financial settlements to be made but does not allow remarriage.

Many people apply for nullity of their marriage, when they want to remarry, but they are difficult to obtain because the courts do not wish nullity of marriage to become the back door for divorce. Nevertheless, the grounds for the granting of nullity have been extended substantially over the last few years.

Anyone seeking a judicial separation should consult a lawyer familiar with the Irish jurisdiction. However, although the grounds for divorce in England and Wales and the grounds for a judicial separation in Eire are different, Irish people considering the latter option will face many of the same sorts of problems that people going through a divorce do in the UK. For example, difficulties over making arrangements for children and deciding how the couple's assets will be split cause universal problems. Husbands and wives, wherever they live, should consider time and time again, if there is any way they can avoid separation and continue living together as a family – on financial grounds alone.

Men and women who want to remarry after the failure of a marriage usually have only one option – to leave Ireland. Divorce in another country is recognised by the Irish state (although not the church which is Roman Catholic) provided the couple are eligible to be divorced in that country and fulfill the legislative requirements.

Most importantly, a couple considering divorce under UK jurisdiction must have lived in England, Wales or Scotland for a year *before* the petition is filed – not a year before they think the decree absolute will be granted. It is not enough for a couple to come and live in England purely to divorce or to buy a property here and then just come and live in England occasionally. They must be able to prove that they have lived and worked in the UK continuously for at least a year before the petition is filed.

Eileen and Kevin were born and brought up in Dublin. They married there and came to England. Four years later, their marriage failed. Kevin remarried an Englishwoman and continued to live here permanently.

Eileen remarried an Irishman. They first lived in Ireland, then came back to England before that marriage foundered as well. Eileen started divorce proceedings but her second husband argued that he was not properly married to her because her first marriage had not ended legally.

In fact, this was not true, and was a badly disguised ploy by her second husband not to pay her any maintenance. Nevertheless, it does illustrate the care couples who were originally married in Eire must take when they divorce under any part of the UK jurisdiction.

DIVORCE ABROAD

When a couple can be divorced in more than one country serious legal problems can develop. British nationals who live abroad can decide whether to be divorced at home or abroad. What matters is where it makes most sense for them to be divorced, and they should work out which jurisdiction is equally fair to both parties.

One of the factors that will determine where the divorce takes place is who puts a petition in first. This will carry some weight when everything else is finely balanced. So if there is jurisdiction in Britain and another country and you would be better off in Britain, start proceedings quickly.

But if the English courts would favour the husband more than the wife, a judge would be likely to tell them to use the jurisdiction that would be fairest to both. It creates a bad impression on a judge if you, as petitioner, have deliberately opted for the jurisdiction most favourable to you.

One English woman, who had lived in France and was married to a Frenchman, decided to file her petition in the UK. Her husband was able to have the proceedings stopped completely, however, because the judge believed that justice would be served better in France.

An American couple who were married in Italy but had lived in the UK for six years and wanted to divorce could have their case heard in any of the three countries. They could go to the States because they were still domiciled there (in the sense that that was where they came from and where they were both likely to die), but they could also use the English or Italian courts because in the first instance this would be their country of residence and in the second this would be where their assets were. However, even if they had lived in Britain for a few years, if most of their assets were still in Italy it would be more sensible for the divorce to take place there.

Under Moslem law a man divorces his wife simply by saying 'I divorce you' three times, and his liability to his wife is only five gold coins. That is patently unfair for a British woman or, say, an Iranian or an Iraqi living in Britain. While the British courts accept the divorce, it does not preclude the woman from gaining some settlement from her husband's assets in

Britain, provided, of course, he has not taken everything he owns out of the country. British courts can make orders for financial provision when a divorce or separation has taken place abroad, provided permission has been granted by a High Court judge. The judge will only give the go-ahead if he or she considers that the circumstances warrant it – if, for example, the person making the application now lives in Britain.

When a divorce takes place abroad, provided that it was recognized in the country which granted it, it will always be recognized in the UK. This is not always the case in reverse: if a couple were married in a Catholic country (which does not recognize divorce) and they came to live in the UK and subsequently divorce there, UK legislation would only cover them, their dependants and assets in the UK.

We pointed out in Chapter 8 that when assets are held abroad, UK courts have only limited powers to make a husband transfer a share of his assets to his wife, or vice versa, particularly when the money is tied up in the Middle or Far East.

19

*D*O-IT-YOURSELF DIVORCE

Legal fees, as we have emphasized time and time again, can mount up during divorce proceedings, so you and your spouse may be tempted to save money and try to do it yourselves. There is no legal reason why you should not do this, as lawyers have no monopoly on handling divorces.

You may save the legal fees, but you may find the process so time-consuming that it is not worth the effort. It can, for example, take an experienced solicitor about 20 minutes to fill in an unreasonable behaviour petition; an articled clerk might take a couple of hours over the same petition; but it could take you a couple of days, and even then you may not get it right – it could be defended by your spouse or rejected by the judge, in which case you only incur costs for your spouse for which you will have to pay. So it could be a false economy.

Even if you do all the paperwork yourself, we would advise you to consult a sympathetic solicitor to cast his or her eye over what you are doing. While that may cost you about £100, it will be money well spent and he or she should be able to point out some of the pitfalls you can avoid.

The following list is not comprehensive, but will give you a few points to consider before you embark on your own proceedings.

First of all read *Divorce Legal Procedures and Financial Facts* (see Appendix C for details). Also, read a basic legal textbook for trainee solicitors that deals with divorce, which will give you an insight into the way judges operate. Rayden & Jackson on divorce is the divorce lawyers' Bible (see Appendix C for details).

However intelligent you are, unless both parties are prepared to do the divorce themselves, the solicitor acting for one party is likely to end up doing twice as much work as usual, by having to explain to the other party what needs to be done. You may not end up saving that much money.

If you have no children and no assets, apart from a few personal possessions, a do-it-yourself divorce should hold few problems or surprises.

Are you and your spouse in complete agreement on how your assets are to be divided and how you are going to look after the children? If there is one word of dissent you should seek independent legal advice and both be prepared to follow the advice.

Remember that divorce is emotionally charged. Are you sure that each of you is sufficiently dispassionate about what you are undertaking to come to an equitable arrangement? One of a good solicitor's most useful functions is to take the heat out of the process and to explain each stage of the process calmly. Even when solicitors do their own divorces they tend to make a mess of them, because of the emotional factors involved.

Are you considering divorce on grounds of unreasonable behaviour? If so, we strongly advise you to consult a solicitor. An unreasonable behaviour petition is difficult at the best of times and not something for an amateur to consider. A do-it-yourself divorce should be restricted to simple adultery petitions, or two- or five-year separations. Other grounds may be tricky, not least because you are likely to be on bad terms with your spouse.

Spouses must try to make sure that capital claims against them are dismissed. You might otherwise find that another application is launched for an increase of funds, and while you may have been in amicable agreement when you were going through your divorce, you may be less well disposed to your former spouse five or ten years later. If a husband has to pay maintenance, an attempt should be made to negotiate it for, say, five years, with an order that his wife's claim will then be dismissed, thus giving her time to find a job and find her feet.

Do you have children? Who pays for their upkeep? Is there a mortgage on the house in which they live? Are they at fee-paying schools? If your answers to these questions assume a continuous source of money, what happens if the source of that money dries up? You may not want to consider such a morbid topic, but you must consider how you and your children would survive if their other parent were to die, or how they would survive if you were to die. Speak to an independent insurance consultant about what life assurance, endowment policies and other insurance you should consider during divorce proceedings (also see Chapter 11).

Are you selling your house? Are you doing the conveyancing yourselves? You should attempt to sort out these financial affairs at the same time as your divorce, so that the agreement can be incorporated into an order on decree nisi, effective, so far as capital is concerned, upon decree absolute.

Once you have considered all these points, draw up a timetable of what you need to do, and when. For example, if you are the respondent you should acknowledge service of the petition within eight days of receiving it. When you start the process for real, you must make sure that you stick to the time limits.

Write down all the forms you will need, what they are for and what details you will need to provide. Ring up your local court to find out where you can obtain standard papers, such as the petition. Forms are, otherwise, available from HMSO.

Do you possess authorized copies of your birth certificate, marriage certificate and any previous marriage certificates? Photocopies are rarely accepted. Contact the Office of Population Censuses and Surveys if you need replacements. If you ask the OPCS to search for you it can be expensive and take some weeks. Consider going to London and doing it yourself (the address is given in Appendix C).

Make a list of all court charges you will have to pay, and at what stage they will have to be paid.

Keep a copy of every document you write and receive, particularly letters between you and your spouse, and any informal lists you draw up of your expenditure and income.

Only when you have gathered all the information you need and the documents which you will have to complete, and have a clear idea of what you need to do and when, should one of you file the petition.

When negotiating with your spouse, particularly when this is being done by correspondence, be sure to mark the top of any letters that include financial offers to settle the matter 'without prejudice' to prevent them being used in the court bundle. If you do not mark them in this way, the judge may see them and take the negotiating offers into account before reaching a decision. If you want to rely on any offer your spouse makes in correspondence so far as costs are concerned, then write on the top 'without prejudice save as to costs' or refer to the case of Calderbank.

$\mathscr{D}$IVORCE MAY NOT BE THE END

People find divorce so stressful that it can be an overwhelming relief to know that decree nisi has been granted and it is just a matter of waiting for decree absolute. This is not always the case, however. We point out in Chapter 22 that divorce can be a mixed blessing, and in this chapter we look at the problems that can develop when divorce proceedings are, in theory, finalized.

For a start, although the majority of divorces are only finalized when the arrangements for the children and the couple's financial affairs have been sorted out, a significant percentage have not sorted out their money problems before decree absolute. And even when an agreement is reached, if the woman's claim has not been dismissed she, and any children of the marriage, may be able to ask the husband/father for more money.

MAINTENANCE

Varying orders
People whose claims have not been dismissed by the court – which covers women who have not remarried and children who are below the age of 18 or who are in full-time education – are entitled to go back to court time and time again to ask for more money. There is a special form for applying for a variation and you will only need to file an affidavit if your spouse ignores the application.

Applications are usually made when inflation has eaten away at the maintenance or, as in the case of children, their needs increase as they grow older. Maintenance can also go up or down if there is a material change in circumstances on either side. If a wife wins the pools, her husband may not have to pay maintenance any more and her claim will be dismissed. If a husband remarries a wealthy woman, his former wife can argue that her maintenance should increase, as we describe later in this chapter.

Other wives can do badly out of maintenance: they may be proud and reluctant to go to court and stir up feelings that have been dormant; a woman may find herself dependent on state benefits if her former husband loses his job or has his working hours reduced. Although the law states which circumstances have to be taken into account, there are no hard-and-fast rules about what increases or reductions will be granted: each case is considered on its own merits and the result will depend on the district judge or magistrate, who hears the application.

Enforcing orders
When a father or husband defaults on maintenance payments – even for a month – his former wife can find herself quickly in debt. The chances are that the money has been allocated for certain items (mortgage, bills, etc.) which have to be met. She no doubt will have considered the payments to be like a salary. Her husband may claim that he can no longer afford to pay her, but he should have gone back to court to ask for the maintenance to be altered, not have stopped paying without warning.

When a wife or mother is genuinely concerned that her husband might not meet his obligations she could register the maintenance order at a magistrates' court. The husband, once the order is registered, then has to make all the payments through that court, which deducts a small handling charge. When the payments are in arrears, the court will automatically follow them up (a divorce county court will not automatically chase missed maintenance payments unless requested).

You should notify the court when a single payment is missed because, as arrears mount up, they become increasingly difficult to claim – simply because of the amount. In extremis, the court can deduct the money from the man's salary, send in the bailiffs to remove some of his possessions to be sold, evict him or – as a last resort – imprison him if he has the means to pay and wilfully refuses to part with the cash. The new Child Agency will help a mother recover maintenance payments for the children. She and her children, in the meantime, will be able to claim state benefit if she has no other income, and the Department of Social Security (DSS) may take up her case.

Cases when a husband who has left his last known address are trickier: a woman may only be able to trace her former husband with the help of the DSS, which may keep a record of an up-to-date address if he is still paying national insurance.

Enforcement orders similar to those in effect in England, Wales and Northern Ireland exist in Scotland, although they have different legal names.

When the husband has no assets in the UK, his wife may be concerned that he will not keep his word about paying maintenance. When the order is made, the court can demand security for the payment. A letter will go to the husband's bank, whether it is in the UK or abroad, explaining that an order of the court requires that sufficient money is always kept in a particular account to cover the maintenance.

There is another circumstance whereby security is often imposed, and that is in relation to the early death of a paying spouse. If there is sufficient money left in the spouse's estate to fulfil his obligations and he is domiciled in the UK, a claim can be brought under the Inheritance (Provision for Family and Dependants) Act 1975 should the husband have failed to make adequate provision in his Will.

Eric had hefty maintenance obligations to his wife and three children; he also had to meet the school fees. The bulk of the family's capital was tied up in the house in which his wife and children lived. One of the terms of the order was that he take out life insurance to protect his family's position should he die while his maintenance obligations were still in existence.

LUMP SUMS

In England, Wales and Northern Ireland lump sum orders cannot be varied. In Scotland, as we explained in Chapter 18, they can only be varied in exceptional circumstances. However, when the money is being paid in instalments, the payer can ask for the frequency of payment to be changed as long as the overall figure is not affected. If the payments are missed and the lump sum is more than £5,000 in total, interest will be payable on the overdue instalments.

CONTACT

Perhaps we should not be surprised that so many fathers lose contact with their children after divorce. As a general rule, only when the couple continue to live in the same area is there a realistic chance that the parent they do not live with (usually the father) will see the children frequently. And, as fathers develop new relationships and possibly have more children, their priorities tend to change.

Even then, when the couple both continue to live in the same area, contact should not present any problems: parents have a choice of whether or not they continue to keep in touch with their children. Children, also, have some say in whether or not they see the absent parent, depending on their ages and how they feel about the divorce.

The problems begin when the mother, for example, meets someone and wants to go and live, say 200 miles from where the father lives, taking the children with her. It is simply bad luck for the father, because the courts will not prevent a former spouse moving away and taking the children, unless it is clearly not in the children's best interests. It is then difficult and expensive for parents and children to keep in touch: if the father goes to them, where is he going to stay? If the children are quite young, who is going to accompany them when they visit their father? In these circumstances, children are likely to visit the absent parent less frequently but for longer periods – or lose touch completely.

Varying and enforcing orders

Contact can be enforced by the court, as long as the children are willing. A mother cannot normally prevent a father from seeing his children, and moreover, for the healthy emotional development of her children, she should encourage them to keep in touch. A father is more likely to continue to pay maintenance if he is closely involved in his children's upbringing. If a mother wilfully takes the children out for the day when the father expects to pick them up, the court, by invitation, will intervene.

Contact cannot be imposed in reverse, however. A mother cannot force a reluctant father to fulfil his obligations to look after the children. The mother cannot demand that the father sees their children for longer periods in school holidays if, say, the father, who has looked after the children every other weekend, meets another woman, or has followed his job to another part of the country. She can only hope that he will want to see them as much as possible.

Complications begin when either parent wants to go abroad. Either party can apply to court, if they cannot agree matters between them, asking for an order permitting the children to be taken out of the jurisdiction, or otherwise. The court may allow the mother to go abroad on condition that she sends the children home once or twice a year to see the father – and pays for the travel. However, if their father has greater means than their mother and/or stepfather, he might be expected to pay the fares. If the children's father is posted abroad and he invites the children to spend the whole of the Easter holidays with him, he may be required to undertake to return the children to their mother before the summer term begins.

KIDNAPPING

The most terrible ordeals can develop when one parent is a foreign national and wants to take the children home to live with his or her family permanently.

We have already pointed out that if a parent wants to take a child out of the UK without the consent of the other parent or an order of the court, he or she may be breaking the law – under the Child Abduction Act 1984. A non-British parent may have no compunction in flouting this law and may believe it is not relevant in the circumstances – the child is going 'home', after all.

If you think your child is likely to be kidnapped, notify the police immediately. Give them a recent photograph and full physical description of the child and the likely abductor so that officials at ports and airports can look out for them. You should then consider making your child a ward of court, or applying for an appropriate order under the Children Act, thus making your spouse in breach of any order made in those proceedings if he or she attempts to take the child out of England or Wales (similar laws exist in Scotland and Northern Ireland).

If your child disappears or fails to come home after a holiday abroad, you are right to fear the worst: it is extremely difficult to get a child back. While copies of the English orders will be sent to the country to which the child has been abducted, it is up to officers of the foreign court to trace the child and demand that he or she be returned to the UK. Such difficulties most commonly arise between UK women and Asian or Far Eastern men, who have a more dominant role in society. If a man wants to take his children home, he will do so, without any questions being asked. There is a Charity called *Reunite* and a network of international lawyers who will help in these kinds of situations, and the Foreign Office will assist, but there are limits to what they can achieve. Legal aid is available to anyone who wants it in these situations.

PARENTAL ILLNESS

It can happen that the parent with whom the children are living becomes very ill, either physically or mentally. In those circumstances the other parent may agree to take over the day-to-day care of the children, or to see them more often. If there is no agreement, it is always possible for a parent to apply to the court for a residence order in his or her favour. If there is a serious problem and the second parent cannot help, the Social Services may become involved.

HOMOSEXUAL AND LESBIAN RELATIONSHIPS

If the parent who has the children living with him or her is in a homosexual relationship, this need not provide any grounds for the arrangements for the children to be altered. The bottom line is how well the children are being looked after, and who is to say that the parent's care of the children will necessarily be impaired by his or her new relationship? Similarly, a father who has contact with his children and is a practising homosexual will not, by virtue of that, be prevented from seeing his children. Children have a right to know their parents.

SEPARATION AGREEMENTS

Separation agreements can be enforced if your spouse becomes reluctant to stick to his or her side of the bargain. However, you have to do this through a civil claim in the Queen's Bench Division or the county court – not through divorce legislation. Judges are usually keen that the terms of the separation agreement are maintained, particularly when both spouses received independent legal advice.

REMARRIAGE

When divorced people meet another partner – whether it is before divorce proceedings begin, a few months after decree absolute, or some years later – their financial means will change again, sometimes to their advantage, often not. The new couple then have to decide whether to marry again or cohabit. The decision is not, of course, always based on money: there are plenty of people who are only prepared to share a house with someone to whom they are married, but considering the financial implications of the new relationship can make a difference.

Couples should always aim at a clean break, because they then will not have the former wife or husband to think about. But remember: only the very rich can support two households and, sadly, many second marriages founder in part because of the financial strain.

WOMEN

Rose suddenly decided to leave Guy after 13 years of marriage when she fell in love with an old family friend, Jeremy, and took her three children to live with him. Guy was sure that she was going to marry Jeremy and thought that he should only have to pay maintenance to Rose for a few months.

They agreed in the end that she should receive a reasonable lump sum in order to buy a house for the children, but it was a much smaller sum than Rose had expected. Her solicitor argued that Jeremy might suddenly decide not to marry Rose after all (or even be run over before they married, or indeed might not maintain her), and she therefore should expect maintenance for a further limited period to give her time to find her feet. Guy's solicitor, on the other hand, said that the evidence was overwhelming that she would remarry, so the element in the lump sum, for capitalization of her maintenance payments for the future, was tiny. She agreed to maintenance for a year and dismissal of all her claims for financial relief.

MEN

Gerard was desperate to remarry but Nicola refused to start divorce proceedings until he had agreed to give her the house completely. She argued that she had nothing else from the marriage. Gerard reluctantly agreed, preferring that solution to a battle in court, even though a district judge would have ordered the house to be sold and a fairer division made. Gerard felt that it might have taken a year to sort the problem out through the court, that he would have to pay the mortgage all that time, and that he might as well get it over as quickly as possible, give Nicola the house as a lump sum and start again.

When the parties cannot afford a clean break, the bitterness can continue for years. When a man remarries a wealthy woman or his business starts to do well, his former wife is entitled to go back to the court to have her maintenance payments increased and her reasonable needs catered for. The court may agree with the first wife's claim on the grounds that her husband's outgoings have become a smaller proportion of his income and that she should benefit.

This can be a real irritation for the second wife who does not see why she should have to support her husband's first wife and children. The new wife's income is not directly relevant to the former wife's maintenance payments, in that a judge cannot make orders in favour of the first wife against the second.

Where it becomes relevant is when the second wife's income relieves the husband of obligations that he previously had to meet. If household bills, for example, are now shared, it leaves more income available for the first wife to claim against.

Many second marriages founder when the second wife realizes that she would be better off without her husband, especially if she has a successful career, is earning a good salary and the first wife is at home looking after the children (apparently living off her, albeit indirectly).

The children of his first marriage are a father's prime responsibility; if he takes on other responsibilities that is his choice. However, there are occasional exceptions. One father, who had taken on a huge second mortgage, could no longer support the children of his first marriage when interest rates started to rise. He applied for a reduction in the maintenance payments he had to make, the Court of Appeal found in his favour, and his children had to live on state benefits.

CHILDREN

Former wives do not always do well, of course, out of their husband's second marriages. When a husband marries a younger woman who is not earning but looking after the children of the second marriage, the husband can argue that maintenance to a first wife whose children have grown up should be reduced because his primary obligation is to his younger children.

Second husbands often feel aggrieved because while they have no formal financial responsibility for the children of their wife's first marriage, there will be some day-to-day expenditure from which the children will benefit. When second husbands have children of their own, they may resent spending any money on their step-children, preferring to spend it on their own children.

COHABITATION AFTER DIVORCE

Bearing in mind the difficulties of second marriages, cohabitation may seem preferable, in the short term, although in the long term you have little security, as we pointed out in Chapter 17.

Lawrence was thrilled when his former wife, Veronica, started to live with Duncan five years after their marriage ended: at last, he saw an end to his responsibility to her. However, the twist in this tale was that Duncan was an undischarged bankrupt, and he and Veronica decided not to marry. Lawrence was incensed, and told his solicitor that he refused to continue paying maintenance as it would mean he'd be supporting Duncan as well.

Lawrence's solicitor had a difficult job persuading him not to waste money in court. If he made life too difficult for Veronica, she would probably force Duncan out. Lawrence would then be back to square one. In time, Duncan would be discharged from his bankruptcy, might marry Veronica, and Lawrence's obligations would come to an end, leaving him with a clear conscience. The moral is that you should hesitate to rush in and demand a reduction in maintenance payments immediately your wife is cohabiting with someone.

Cohabitation can also be advantageous for a man who is supporting another family. When a second marriage fails, he may have to try to contribute to two additional households, as well as surviving himself. If he had merely cohabited with his second wife, his obligations to her in law would have been less – whatever his moral obligations.

One solicitor, who had been kept busy with a wealthy man's emotional misfortunes, advised him – after his third marriage had failed – to live with his fourth partner and her child and not attempt to marry her, and see whether or not the relationship had a long-term future.

21
$\mathscr{N}$ULLITY OF MARRIAGE

An alternative to divorce is to seek a decree of nullity of marriage. You may want to do this if you have religious objections to divorce or if for some other reason you wish to have a court declare that your marriage never existed, or no longer exists.

There are two types of nullity decree. One, which declares your marriage void (that is, that it never existed), can be obtained only on proof of certain grounds. These are limited to matters that are contrary to the concept of marriage as embodied in English law. They include under-age and bigamous marriages, marriages between persons of the same sex, and marriages between persons who are closely related, for example, if a man were to marry his brother's daughter. The second is a decree that declares your marriage void from the date of the decree. It is thus similar to, though technically distinct from, a decree of divorce. This second type of decree is available on proof that one of the parties did not consent to the marriage or on proof of one of the partner's wilful refusal, or incapacity, to consummate the marriage. A decree of the first sort may be obtained by anyone who has a financial interest in the marriage; only a party to the marriage can obtain a decree of the second sort, which might be based on grounds of the man's impotence, for example. In either case, the court has exactly the same powers to make orders relating to money, property and children as does a divorce court.

Nullity decrees are not often used, but they can become important when arguments arise over inheritance or pension rights, where the validity of a marriage can be crucially important. For example, if a woman is pregnant with another man's child, and conceals this fact, the marriage can be annulled.

There are popular misconceptions about the state of the parties at the time of the marriage, *vis-á-vis* annulment. If a man is so drunk that he is unaware that he is being taken to a registry to be married, he can later argue for annulment. However, the chances are that if he'd been that drunk he would not have been able to say anything or to go through with the wedding ceremony.

22

RECONCILIATION AND CONCILIATION

Many people confuse the two words 'reconciliation' and 'conciliation'. The misunderstanding is so rife that the National Family Conciliation Council changed its name in 1992 to the National Association of Mediation Services.

'Reconciliation' applies if a marriage has hit a rocky patch – the husband and wife may even have separated – but each partner hopes to be able to salvage the relationship. Time to think, sessions with a marriage guidance counsellor or talking to friends and each other may enable them to stay together.

'Conciliation' or 'mediation' on the other hand usually refers to the help that couples receive when their marriage has irretrievably broken down, but when they are still more or less on speaking terms. Instead of discussing their plans for the children (and their money and property) through solicitors, they turn first to the conciliation service, which provides neutral territory to work out the best options.

Conciliation does not, of course, preclude reconciliation. A handful of couples realize when they are sorting out their affairs that they and their children will be much better off – both financially and emotionally – if the family stays together.

RECONCILIATION AND OTHER SUPPORT SERVICES

We have emphasized throughout this guide that divorce has little to recommend it. Unless you are wealthy, or young with no children and few assets, you are likely to be much poorer after a divorce – both emotionally and financially. When the petition for divorce is filed you have to submit a 'certificate of reconciliation' which declares whether or not you have discussed reconciliation. It is a mistake not to attempt reconciliation at some stage, but the certificate is only a formality. Perhaps judges should question couples closely to find out what they have done to keep their marriage going but, at the moment, this plays no formal part in divorce proceedings.

When you have pre-school or school-age children we would urge you to think again and again before embarking on divorce. The divorce will inevitably damage them and you must question seriously whether it is really worth putting their stability and future happiness at risk by putting your own feelings before theirs.

Many people believe that a couple who are constantly arguing will harm their children more if they were to stay together. We do not know whether or not this is true. Certainly for some families, divorce is the lesser of two evils but the majority of children, whether it is a year, five years or ten years after their parents' divorce, wish their parents had stayed married. Laura is 27, and her parents divorced when she was 11; although she knows intellectually that their marriage is over, she still dreams and looks forward to the day when they will live together again.

Divorce is difficult, whether or not you are aiming at reconciliation. It is hard emotional work and most people need some help, either as a couple or individually. There are a number of options, depending on the support you need. A number of solicitors who specialize in family law are beginning to appreciate the value of having a counsellor attached to their firms, but there are only a handful who have one on a permanent basis.

Marriage guidance

The best known organization is Relate, formerly called the Marriage Guidance Council. In addition, there are a number of similar organizations affiliated to different faiths.

Some branches have waiting lists as long as four months, although it depends both on the time of year you approach the organization, on local demand and on your own availability: if you can only go at 6 p.m. on Fridays you may have to wait for many months. However, you should be able to have an initial interview sooner than this.

Some people do not continue after the first interview. Of those who commit themselves to a number of sessions, the average is just over six. In 1991, for example, there were 60,000 initial interviews; and 40,000 booked sessions. Between 40 and 45 per cent went as couples; the majority of people who went on their own were women.

Relate estimates that about 15 per cent of those who go to see a counsellor intending to divorce change their minds, although a similar number who go with an open mind eventually decide to divorce. The majority have already decided what they want to do.

Costs

There are no fixed fees; clients are asked to contribute up to £20 a session although on average they pay £10, and nothing if they are unemployed.

EMOTIONAL AND PSYCHOLOGICAL SUPPORT

The temptation to ask your solicitor to help you unravel your marriage emotionally, as well as financially and legally, can be overwhelming. We have stressed how expensive a solicitor's time is, and also explained that he or she is not qualified to help you in this way, though many of the more experienced divorce solicitors can assist and consider it part of the service. When you need more specific support you must find someone equipped to help.

You may be clinically depressed or you may simply want to understand what went wrong; how you contributed to the breakdown of the marriage because, as much as you might like to deny it, it takes two to make a relationship and two to break it. You may also want to make sure that you do not repeat the same mistake again and fall for a person with a similar personality to your spouse, or you may want to minimize the psychological damage that the divorce will have on your children.

You could be helped by any of the following: a counsellor, a psychoanalyst, a psychologist or a therapist. Your general practitioner may have a counsellor or therapist attached to his or her practice. If you are seriously depressed, you may be referred to a psychiatrist or a hospital psychologist – both work within the National Health Service. Friends may be able to put you in touch with a local private counsellor or therapist.

Your GP should be able to advise you in the first instance and certainly will help you if you are clinically depressed. But if you are confused by the options, contact one of the organizations listed in Appendix C, to point you in the right direction.

Costs

Some professionals work through the NHS; many more are private and charge between £10 and £30 an hour. You may see a counsellor for one session; you could see a therapist for a dozen sessions; you could see a psychoanalyst for years.

CONCILIATION

A small proportion of people who are likely to divorce consult the conciliation or mediation service to help them sort out the options before they consult a solicitor. Members of the National Association of Meditation and Conciliation Services can help couples decide how their children can best be cared for after the divorce; members of the Family Mediation Service can also help couples unravel their finances and decide what to do with their property.

This is separate from in-court conciliation, which we described briefly in Chapter 9. When parents cannot decide how their children are to be looked after, the court welfare officer will interview them – and their children, unless they are very young – and produce a report which the judge will use to decide the best arrangements.

The idea behind voluntary conciliation, or mediation, is it can help the couple can sort out their affairs in neutral surroundings with impartial assistance. A mediator will only guide them, the decisions have to be made by the couple, but they are made in a spirit of co-operation, which is often absent if the parents negotiate via solicitors. Mediators, as a result, are keen to retain their autonomy and remain independent of the judicial process.

Usually, the couple will discuss their affairs with one or two mediators. Occasionally, feelings run so high that the mediators will talk to the husband and wife in separate rooms, providing 'shuttle diplomacy'. Mediators are trained counsellors and will treat all information in confidence.

The National Association of Mediation and Conciliation Services aims to help parents resolve their differences over their children in a logical manner so that when problems arise in the future, as they inevitably do when children grow up, their parents will be equipped to sort out the problems themselves. Members of the Association do not pretend that mediation will mean that a husband hates his wife less or she trusts him more, but that they will learn how to deal with each other.

Your solicitor may recommend that you see a mediator, or you can contact one yourself. Increasingly, because of the demands of the Children Act, it is expected that judges will recommend that couples seek voluntary mediation before the in-court procedures have to be invoked.

If you use the Family Mediation Association, they provide two mediators: an experienced family lawyer and a counsellor experienced in marital and family work. The combination of two people with different professional backgrounds gives couples the opportunity to consider all the problems they face: over their children, the family home, money, separation and divorce. The mediators help couples work out a framework for their individual futures and their children's.

Ken and Deborah were still living in the same house when they consulted mediators. They had a 10-year old daughter and an 8-year old son who seemed to bicker more than most children. They knew that separation was inevitable, and had considered taking one child each and/or that Ken should go back to Canada where his family lived. After two sessions, they both agreed that the children should be involved in the process. Both of the children wanted their father to stay in England and it emerged that their son depended on Ken much more than either he or Deborah appreciated. While the children might have made their feelings known if they had just used solicitors, Ken and Deborah both believe that the mediators reduced the stress in deciding what arrangements were best for the whole family.

Advocates of the conciliation services claim that their service saves costs. But this is controversial. It reduces the legal costs for those who use it but, at the moment, the service can only help a few thousand couples a year. Were it available for all divorcing couples it would be expensive to run. In 1990, for example, only 3,500 couples were able to use the services offered by the National Association – a tiny percentage of the total number of divorces (191,615 in England and Wales in 1990) although, of course, not every couple needs a mediator.

Costs

There are no fixed fees for using the mediation services. Clients using the services of the National Association will be asked for a contribution per session. It is usually £25, or £1 per £1,000 income. It may be possible to claim a small sum for mediation under the legal aid scheme. Clients usually see mediators two or three times.

Members of the Family Mediation Association charge between £40 and £60 an hour. A session lasts about an hour and a half, and a settlement can be reached within three and six sessions. Felicity and Roger reached a settlement after four and a half hours with a mediator, which cost them both £180. Their solicitors had estimated costs of £10,000 each if they went to court.

There are some parts of the country where mediators are not available (for examples, parts of Wales, the North West and Cornwall). Contact the organizations listed in Appendix C for details of your nearest branch.

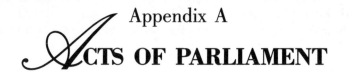

Appendix A

ACTS OF PARLIAMENT

MARRIED WOMEN'S PROPERTY ACT 1882
Section 17 enables the court to rule on the property rights of husbands and wives, and could be of use to one party if the other was, for example, going bankrupt.

LAW OF PROPERTY ACT 1925
Section 30 enables a cohabiting man or woman to apply for the sale of a property which he or she co-owns with his or her partner.

MATRIMONIAL CAUSES ACT 1973
Still the central legislation for divorce. Sets out how a divorce can be obtained. Sets out at Section 41 the procedure for the Children Appointments (if for some reason the judge is not satisfied with the proposed arrangements for the children. Since the implementation of the Children Act 1989, these appointments are no longer compulsory). Explains what financial orders can be made by the court and what considerations the court will take into account in deciding financial relief issues.

INHERITANCE (PROVISION FOR FAMILY AND DEPENDANTS) ACT 1975
Provides the jurisdiction to enable a dependant to make a claim against the estate of a deceased person who does not leave reasonable provision for the claimant in his or her Will.

DOMESTIC VIOLENCE AND MATRIMONIAL PROCEEDINGS ACT 1976
One of the Acts enabling a cohabitee/spouse to apply for injunctions ordering the other party to get out of the house, or to stop assaulting him or her.

CHILD ABDUCTION ACT 1984
Establishes criminal sanctions in relation to children taken out of the jurisdiction.

MATRIMONIAL AND FAMILY PROCEEDINGS ACT 1984
'Updated' the Matrimonial Causes Act 1973. Made clean breaks more likely. Enables people divorced out of England and Wales jurisdiction to apply for financial relief in England and Wales.

CHILDREN ACT 1989
Provides a framework of legislation for all matters relating to children, including residence and contact; and finances.

CHILD SUPPORT ACT 1991
Provides for a way of dealing with maintenance payments for children.

Appendix B

GLOSSARY OF LEGAL TERMS AND SAMPLE PETITION FORM

Adultery
Consensual sexual intercourse between a married person and a person of the opposite sex during the marriage.

Ancillary relief
The whole range of financial orders which can be made by the court following an application by either the husband or the wife.

Care and control
The description of the powers which used to be given to the parent who looked after the children. Orders for care and control can only be made if an application for this was filed before 14th October 1991.

Decree absolute
The final end of the marriage.

Decree nisi
The first decree of divorce. Entitles the petitioner to apply for a decree absolute after six weeks and a day.

Domicile
Normally the country in which you are settled. It is possible however to have a country of domicile which is different from the country you live in. Consult your lawyer!

Financial disclosure
Producing a summary of the financial position of a spouse.

Green form
The form filled in by someone seeking legal aid, to enable initial advice to be given.

Injunction
An order for someone to do something or to stop doing something.

Petitioner
The person who applies for a divorce or judicial separation.

Prayer
An application (e.g. for costs).

Registrar (now superseded by district judge)
A judge in a district registry.

Residence orders
Orders settling the arrangements to be made as to the person with whom a child is to live.

Respondent
The person on the receiving end of a petition.

Section 8 order
Any one of the following orders:
(a) a contract order
(b) a prohibited steps order
(c) a residence order
(d) a specific issue order

Section 41 appointment
Appointment where a judge considers the arrangements for the children.

Special procedure divorce
A normal undefended 'quickie' divorce.

Statutory charge
The charge on money or property gained or preserved by any legally aided party, equivalent to his/her legal costs.

IN THE   GUILDFORD COUNTY COURT
PRINCIPAL REGISTRY

No. of Matter

THE PETITION OF   HENRY ANTHONY HANDSOME

Shows that

1. On the 1st day of January 1980 the Petitioner

Henry Anthony Handsome was lawfully married to Barbara Beatrice Handsome (hereinafter called the Respondent) at the Parish Church in the parish of Christ Church Guildford in the County of Surrey

2. The Petitioner and the Respondent last lived together as husband and wife at 1 Acacia Avenue, Guildford in the County of Surre

3. The Petitioner is domiciled in England and Wales

the Petitioner is a Chartered Accountant and resides at

1 Acacia Avenue, Guildford apersaid

and the Respondent is an Aromatherapist and resides at

2 Voluminar Villas, Verney Rd, Colchester in the County Esse

4. There is (are) two children of the family now living namely David Daniel Handsome born on 2nd February 19 and Emma Emerald Handsome, born on 3rd March 19

5. No other child now living has been born to the Respondent during the marriage so far as is known to the Petitioner

6. There are or have been no other proceedings in any court in England and Wales or elsewhere with reference to the marriage or to any children of the family or between the Petitioner and the Respondent with reference to any property of either or both of them

Sample petition: Husband's petition (grounds of adultery)

7. There are no proceedings continuing in any country outside England and Wales which relate to the marriage or are capable of affecting its validity or subsistence

8. The said marriage has broken down irretrievably.

9. The Respondent has committed adultery with a man whose identity is not known to the petitioner and the Petitioner find it intolerable to live with the Respondent.

10. On the 4th day of April 1992 at 2 Voluminous Villas, Verney Rd, Colchester apersaid the Respondent committed adultery ~~with the said~~ and the adultery is continuing

The Petitioner therefore prays:–

    (1) That the said marriage may be dissolved;

    (2) That the Respondent /and/ /~~Co-Respondent~~/ may be ordered to pay the costs of this suit;

    (3) That he may be granted the following ancillary relief:–

        (i) maintenance pending suit

        (ii) a periodical payments order

        (iii) a secured periodical payments order

        (iv) a property adjustment order

(Signed) Grateful & Co

The names and addresses of the persons who are to be served with this Petition are:–

(Respondent) Barbara Beatrice Handsome, c/o her solicitors Jolley & Co, 5 Basildon Rd, Colchester Essex

[(Co-Respondent)]

The Petitioner's address for service is:–

Grateful & Co (REFERENCE FSS/SJB) 6 Farnham Rd Guildford Surrey

    Dated this 6th day of June 1992

Appendix C

FURTHER READING AND USEFUL ADDRESSES

FURTHER READING

The Consumers' Association, *Divorce Legal Procedures and Financial Facts* (Hodder and Stoughton, 1989 – revised edition 1992).

Considers every legal eventuality; gives a comprehensive sequence of divorce proceedings which you could follow for guidance.

J. Dewar, *Law and the Family* (Butterworths, 1992).

Rayden and Jackson, *Divorce and Family Matters* (Butterworths, 1991).

(Some firms of accountants also produce pamphlets on taxation and divorce.)

USEFUL ADDRESSES

General Register Office/OPCS
St Catherine's House
10 Kingsway
London WC2B 6JP
Tel. 071–242 0262
For a certified copy of your birth or marriage certificate(s).

The Law Society
Legal Practice Information
Department
113 Chancery Lane
London WC2A 1PL
Tel. 071–242 1222

Solicitors' Complaints Bureau
Portland House
Stag Place
London SW1E 5BL
Tel. 071–834 2288

Solicitors Family Law Association
Mary I'Anson, Permanent Secretary
24 Croydon Road,
Keston,
Kent BR2 6EJ
Tel. 0689 50227

Legal Aid

The Legal Aid Board
Fifth and Sixth Floors
29/37 Red Lion Street
London WC1R 4PP
Tel. 071–831 4209

The Scottish Legal Aid Board
44 Drumsheugh Gardens
Edinburgh EH3 7SW
Tel. 031–226 7161

Incorporated Law Society of
Northern Ireland
Legal Aid Department
Bedford House
16–22 Bedford Street
Belfast BT2 7FL
Tel. 0232 246441

Marriage guidance services

Catholic Marriage Advisory Council
Clitherow House
1 Blythe Mews
Blythe Road
London W14 0NW
Tel. 071-371 1341

Jewish Marriage Council
23 Ravenshurst Avenue
London NW4 4EE
Tel. 081-203 6311

Relate (or Marriage Guidance
Council)
Local branches are listed in the
telephone directory. If you have
difficulties, contact the
headquarters of the National
Marriage Guidance Council at:
Herbert Gray College
Little Church Street
Rugby
Warwickshire CV21 3AP
Tel. 0788 73241

Scottish Marriage Guidance Council
26 Frederick Street
Edinburgh EH2 2JR
Tel. 031-225 5006

Counselling

This list is far from comprehensive,
but should give you some guidance
in finding appropriate help.
British Association for Counselling
37A Sheep Street
Rugby
Warwickshire CV21 3BX
Tel. 0788 578328

Publishes directories listing
individual counsellors and
counselling agencies.

British Association of
Psychotherapists
37 Maplesbury Road
London NW2 4HJ
Tel. 081-452 9823

Family Welfare Association
501 Kingsland Road
London E8 4AU
Tel. 071-254 6251

Conciliation services

The National Association of
Mediation and Conciliation Services
(formerly The National Family
Conciliation Council)
Shaftesbury Centre
Percy Street
Swindon
Tel. 0793 514055
Concentrates on arrangements for
children.

Family Mediators Association
The Old House
Rectory Gardens
Henbury
Bristol BS10 7AQ
Tel. 0272 500140
Tackles differences over children,
finances and property, including
pensions rights.

The National Association of
Mediation and Conciliation Services
(Scotland)
127 Rose Street
South Lane
Edinburgh EH2 4BB
Tel. 031-220 1610

Also contact the Scottish Law
Society who can put you in touch
with mediator who will help you
resolve your disputes over money
and property:
26 Drumsheugh Gardens
Edinburgh EH3 7YR
Tel. 031 – 225 2050

$\mathcal{I}$NDEX

acknowledgement (of petition) 33
Acts of Parliament 163-4
addresses, useful 168-70
adultery 13, 27-8, 46, 118
affidavit 33, 107-8
age gap 53
alternatives (to divorce) 17
appeals 48
assets, division of 58-60, 75-7
  matrimonial home 58-60

barristers 110-11
bitterness 53-4, 58, 100-1
blame 11-3

Calderbank Letter 119
charge on property 42-3, 89
Child Support Act 1991 82-3
childless couples 49-62
  financial arrangements 49-62
children 13, 63-73, 101, 104-5, 109, 110,
    133-4, 153
  financial arrangements 74-83
  legal situation 64-6
  practical arrangements 63-73
    adult children 69
    contact arrangements 67-8
    contact orders 64
    education 70
    older children 68-9
    residence agreements 71-3
    welfare officers 70-1
    young children 67-8
Children Act 1989 64
clean break 51-4, 60
  vs. maintenance 55-6
cohabitation 132-4
  children 134-5

  financial arrangements 153-4
contact 148-50
counselling 15-6
court appearances 107-14
  barristers 110-1
  how to behave 111-3
  reasons for 107-10
  what happens 113-4
credit cards 44

death in service benefit 90
decree absolute 11, 13, 14, 34
decree nisi 33-4, 35
desertion 13, 30
disclosure, fear of 102-4
division of assets 58-60
*Divorce Legal Procedures and Financial
    Facts* 143
Divorce Reform Act 12
do-it-yourself divorce 18, 137, 143-5

Eire 139-40
emotional advice 24-5, 159

fault 11-3
financial arrangements
  family company and estate 97-9
  heirlooms 93-5
  liquid assets abroad 99
  perks 96-7
  trusts 95-7
financial arrangements, children 74-83
  changing needs 80-1
  Child Support Act 1991 82-3
  education 81
  maintenance 77-80
  splitting up home 75-7
financial arrangements, cohabitation 133-4

financial arrangements, final
  childless couples 49-62
  clean break 51-4
  principle of need 51
financial arrangements, interim 42-5
freezing assets 42
fully-entitled wife 56-7

grounds for divorce, 27-31
  adultery 13, 27-8
  desertion 30
  separation 30-1
  unreasonable behaviour 28-30

home 58-60, 75-7
  family 75-7
  matrimonial 58-60

illness 151
information for solicitor 37-40
  expenditure 39-40
  financial 38-9
  general 38
Inheritance Act 1975 90
injunction 45-6
insurance policies 91
interim orders 42-6
  financial 42-5
  violence 45-6

kidnapping 150-1

Law Commission 13-4
Legal Aid 122-9
  entitlement to 126-7
  statutory charge 127-9
  what is it 123-4
Legal Advice and Assistance 124-6
  abroad 141-2
  entitlement to 124
  entitlements under 125-6
  in Eire 139-40
  in Northern Ireland 136
  in Scotland 136-9
legal aspects of divorce 26-35
  children 64-6
  grounds 27-31
  paperwork 31-5
  when 27-8

legal costs 115-21
  how much 115-7
  keeping down 120-1
  taxation 119-20
  who pays 117-20
life assurance 84-92
lump sums 148

maintenance 44-5, 49-62, 118, 146-8
  children 72-80, 89
  tax 82-3
maintenance pending suit 42
Married Women's Property Act 1882 59
Matrimonial Causes Act 1973 50
  Section 10, 90
Matrimonial and Family Proceedings Act
  1984 51
matrimonial home 58-60
men, post-divorce 152-3
misapprehensions 100-6
  children 104-5
  money 101-4
  residency 100-1
mixed arrangements 61

normal spending patterns 44-5
Northern Ireland 136
nullity of marriage 155-6

'one-third approach' 50

pensions 57-8, 84-92
  clean break 86-7
  flexible schemes 86
  payment of lump sums 87-9
  severe hardship 90
petition 11, 31-3, 166
  form 166
post-divorce 146-54
  children 153
  cohabitation 154
  contracts 148
  illness 151
  kidnapping 150
  lump sums 148
  maintenance 146
  men 152-3
  remarriage 151-2
  women 152

pre-marriage contracts 134-5
principle of need 80-1
pros and cons of divorce 16-7

reconciliation 15, 23, 47-8, 157-62
  conciliation 160-2
  emotional support 159
  support services 157-9
remarriage 151
residence agreements 71-3
residence orders 64
rich couples, options for 60-1
Road to Divorce, England 1530-1987 12

Scotland 136-9
Scottish Family Law Association 19
semi-fully-entitled wife 57-8
separation agreements 151
solicitors 18-23
  changing 22
  choosing 19-21
  finding 18-9
  information required by 37-40
  questions to ask 21-2
  role of 23-5
Solicitors Family Law Association 19, 20
specific issue orders 65
state pension 91-2
statutory charge 128-9
Stone, Laurence 12

tax on maintenance 62-3
tax relief 56

unreasonable behaviour 13, 28-30, 118

violence 45-6

welfare offices 71
wills 91
women 11-2, 13, 19, 82, 84-5, 118, 152
  older 87, 89